RIGHT ON: FROM BLUES TO SOUL IN BLACK AMERICA

Eddison Blues Books *Edited by TONY RUSSELL*

RIGHT ON: FROM BLUES TO SOUL IN BLACK AMERICA

MICHAEL HARALAMBOS

EDDISON PRESS LTD
London

Published by Eddison Press Ltd
2 Greycoat Place, London SW1

© Michael Haralambos 1974

ISBN 0 85649 016 4

I.B.M. Computer Typesetting by Print Origination,
Orrell Mount, Hawthorne Road, Bootle, Lancs.
Printed in Great Britain by
Biddles of Guildford

Contents

Acknowledgements

A large part of the field research for this book was conducted in 1968 with the aid of a grant from the Hill Family Foundation. I am very grateful to the Foundation and to Professor Luther P. Gerlach of the Department of Anthropology, University of Minnesota, who made it possible for me to receive the grant.

My approach to the subject has been influenced by my studies in Anthropology at the University of Minnesota. I should like to thank Professor E. Adamson Hoebel for the opportunity to study at Minnesota. His kindness will always be remembered. I should also like to express my gratitude to the other staff members of the Anthropology Department, in particular to Professor Robert F. Spencer and Professor Pertti J. Pelto.

My sincere thanks go to the black Americans who contributed directly to this book, to the disc-jockeys, singers, musicians and to the many people who assisted in my research in Minneapolis, Chicago, Detroit and New York. Without their support the field-work could not have been conducted.

To those who helped with the discography, Mike Leadbitter, Clive Richardson, Chris Savory and Jim Wilson, I express my appreciation. I am indebted to the record companies and management agencies who provided photographs. I am grateful to Roy Simonds for his kind assistance with illustrations. Particular thanks are due to Bill Greensmith, Paul Oliver and Jeff Titon for the use of the fine photographs taken by themselves. Special thanks also go to Ken Roberts for the loan of records and his continuing interest and encouragement. I gratefully acknowledge the skill and advice of my editor, Tony Russell.

Finally, I should like to express my gratitude to my mother for her unwavering support.

Michael Haralambos, 1974.

Introduction

Our concern in this book is an explanation of changes in black American music, in particular of the decline in popularity of blues and the rise in popularity of soul music. We discover an integral relationship between black society and culture and black music. We argue that changes in the latter can only be understood in association with changes in the former.

Styles of music, like other art forms, never find universal support. There is no such thing as pure art, which, by definition, would transcend the barriers of time and space, override the frontiers of cultures and subcultures, and satisfy that presumed common denominator of mankind, the human spirit. If such a universal as the human spirit exists, an art form has yet to be invented that will reach out and touch it. We find, in practice, that particular kinds of art provide particular kinds of audiences with particular forms of enjoyment and satisfaction. This is a fairly obvious statement, but its implications are too often ignored in the study of music. The major implication is that we must study the audience as well as the music. With this knowledge, we may examine the relationship between audience and music, and observe whether or not there is a concurrent change in the nature of the music and the circumstances of the audience.

The evidence presented in this book suggests there is a concurrent change. A case is made for a mutually dependent relationship of music and society. It therefore follows that music and society, in their mutual cause and effect, change together. However, there are two arguments which may tend to refute the validity of this thesis. The first states that though a particular style of music may originate as a response to a particular social context, when that context changes, the style will continue. This argument assumes that performers and audience become committed to a particular style, and this commitment overrides changes in the social situation. Thus, although a style may at a particular time be largely unrelated to other aspects of society, it is maintained solely because prior conditioning of performers and audience has been sufficiently effective to ensure its maintenance. There is some evidence to support this argument. Taking blues as an example, we find, especially amongst performers, a desire to maintain the style, despite the fact that the social conditions to which it is adapted are fast disappearing. Related to this desire is the fact that many blues singers have become so specialised that they can only perform in terms of the one style. This case for the primacy of prior conditioning may, in part, account for the present-day survival of blues. However, since the number of professional blues singers and the size of their audience is rapidly dwindling, this argument does not contravene our major thesis.

The second argument, which in part runs counter to our major thesis, assumes that a style, by its very nature, has a limited life expectancy. A style, by definition, is a limitation of form within which there are permitted variations. Once a style has become formalised, that is, its boundaries have become fixed and the rules for variation within them established, it can no longer develop, it can only vary the arrangement of its constituent units. Once all the permitted variations have been exhausted, the style can only repeat its expressions. Assuming the audience does not want mere repetition, the style will then die out. Thus the death of a style is a function of the nature of a style and may be unrelated to concurrent social conditions. The basic assumption of this argument is that a style has a finite number of different expressions. If, for example, a style is defined as the permutations in the arrangement of the numbers one to four, after the twenty-four possible permutations have been effected, the style can no longer express itself in a new form.

Thus the arguments that run counter to our thesis—that the development, maintenance and decline of a style is explained in large part as a function of factors extrinsic to the style itself—run as follows. First, a style is maintained simply because people have been so effectively conditioned to liking it, that, no matter what other factors may tend to undermine and contradict this conditioning, it remains effective. As noted above, this explanation is not well supported by the facts, but it cannot be entirely dismissed. The second argument states that a style has a finite number of different expressions, and once all these expressions have been exhausted, whatever the nature of other aspects of society, the style ends. A new style then begins, develops, becomes formalised, expresses its range of permitted variation and ends. And so the process continues. A style, by its very nature, has a life and death of its own. We now turn to a consideration of this second argument.

In practice, a style never becomes completely formalised. It never reaches a point where it can only vary, that is, rearrange fixed units, but continues to develop until it ends. The development of a style means changing the definition of its boundaries. Thus, if we define as the same style the permutations, not only of the numbers one to four, but also of one to five, we alter the boundaries of the style. A brand new unit—the number five—is introduced into the style. This permits new possibilities for variation of the units, it allows new configurations. The process of changing the definition of the boundaries of a style may continue indefinitely, and the continuity of the style is maintained as long as performers and audience recognise it as being the same style. The analyst may find that, despite the continuous introduction of new units, the style maintains a basic structural unity throughout its life.

Using blues music as an example, we may sketch this process. Since the inception of the style, probably late in the 19th century, blues has retained its structural foundations to the present day. The twelve bar 'blues' framework has remained the basis of the style throughout its life. The most popular form of blues in black America, termed by many 'modern' blues, has incorporated elements that were unknown to the style 20 or 30 years ago. Aspects of jazz and gospel music have been introduced, yet 'modern' blues is still seen, by its supporters and detractors alike, to be directly within the mainstream of the style defined as blues. At the time of writing (January 1972), the best-selling blues record in the black American market is Little Johnny Taylor's *Everybody Knows About My Good Thing (Part 1)*. This record shows a further development of the gospel style of blues singing within the basic blues framework.

Despite the fact that blues is still a developing style, it is steadily decreasing in popularity in black America. There are plenty of blues singers around but very few can make a living from their music. If present trends continue, blues will die out in black America. It will neither have exhausted its potential for development as a style, nor will there be a dearth of singers who can perform in terms of it. It will die out simply because nobody wants to listen to it. A style therefore ends because, for some reason or other, it no longer meets the needs of its audience. There is nothing intrinsic to the nature of a style that brings it to an end.

We must therefore look to the audience as the final arbiter of the fate of a style. We return to our original thesis, that music must be examined in relation to its social-cultural context if we are to explain changes in styles. To present an over-simplified model, particular forms of music respond to particular needs, which are a product of particular social contexts. As the context changes, the needs change and the music changes. However, the process is not simply unidirectional as this model implies.

Like any other aspect of society, music is both cause and effect. It is both a product and a producer of the society of which it is a part. We cannot, therefore, point to some or one part of society as the exclusive agent for change of the whole. However, we can argue that certain factors are more important than others in effecting change, and still retain our model. By assigning priority, we do not deny mutual effect. To sketch a simple example: civil rights issues were not specifically mentioned in soul music until the late 1960s, over ten years after concerted civil rights activity was under way. We can make a strong case for this innovation in the words of soul music as being a product of the civil rights struggle. However, we can also reasonably argue that songs advocating civil rights feed back upon the activity which produced them, and so reinforce it.

Turning to the general relationship of black music and black society, we conclude, from the evidence presented in this book, that music is largely a dependent variable. It reflects rather than directs, it is changed rather than changing anything. However, we maintain that certain styles of black music have, at different times, reinforced and inhibited change in other aspects of society.

In reaching the conclusion that music is largely a dependent variable, we must be careful not to underestimate its significance in black society. It has and still plays a vital role. When a culture defines its music as 'the truth', we should be ill-advised to regard it as peripheral.

1/Changing with the Blues

Black Radio and Blues

Radios across the Minneapolis North Side ghetto are tuned to KUXL, the local black station. Over the closing bars of B.B. King's *Why I Sing The Blues*, the disc-jockey Jack Harris, better known as 'Daddy Soul', says, 'Don't you be walkin' round with a frown on your face. This is the blues, your heritage, be proud of it. This is me sugar, I don't know about you.' Apart from a Lowell Fulsom record, this is the only blues Jack Harris plays on his three-hour show.

In 1968 there were over 100 radio stations programming solely for black audiences and over 500 broadcasting at least two hours a day to black listeners. As one measure for assessing the popularity of blues, surveys were taken of the secular music played by black radio stations in Chicago, Detroit, New York and Minneapolis. The station with the largest share of the black audience in each city was selected, WVON in Chicago, WCHB in Detroit, WWRL in New York and KUXL in Minneapolis. Surveys covered three-week periods during Summer 1968, and for KUXL, a three-week period during Summer 1969. Black disc-jockeys and programme directors identified those records in the survey they considered blues. The results show that WVON played 5 blues out of 61 records; WCHB, 2 out of 52; WWRL, 5 out of 73; KUXL, 4 out of 58. A strict definition of blues would reduce the numbers given by about one third. Included are blues ballads such as *Save Your Love For Me* by Bobby Bland, and blues-oriented soul songs such as *Dark End Of The Street* by Little Milton. Shorter surveys of the music played by the other black radio stations in these cities revealed no significant difference in the proportion of blues. The only stations which cater for minority tastes within the black audience broadcast jazz. This suggests the audience for blues is too small to support a radio station catering for its tastes. Like WVON, 'the station that brought soul to Chicago', black radio goes from strength to strength with an almost uninterrupted format of soul music.

What makes these radio stations a good indicator for black musical tastes? Firstly, an overwhelming proportion of the black public listens almost exclusively to them, as the figures given in Chapter 3 show clearly. Cars in Chicago's South and West Side ghettoes plastered with WVON rear-window stickers reveal the loyalty of the station's audience. Secondly, in such a highly competitive business as commercial radio, stations have to be sensitive to public tastes to stay in business. They are financed by advertising, and the larger their share of the audience, the greater their advertising revenue. WVON's success in playing what the black public wants to hear is reflected in its list of advertisers which ranges from Coca Cola, Lucky Strike and Campbell Soups to the Illinois Bell Telephone Company and Greyhound buses. Thirdly, the radio stations reflect the record-buying habits of the black public. WVON's 'Soul 45', a weekly broadsheet listing the 45 best-selling soul and blues records in Chicago, is compiled from returns from ghetto record shops. All these records are played by the station.

An important source of data for this book is the opinions and assessments of black tastes in music and of black music in general, given by programme directors and disc-jockeys. Why should their views be considered authoritative? Firstly, they are personally as well as economically committed to the music they play. As Ed Cook, a disc-jockey at WVON, puts it, 'I've been in it for eighteen years and I certainly don't think I could be really truthful with myself and my audience if I didn't really like the music. Y'see I have to inject my personality into it.' Secondly, they are in constant touch with their audience. Listeners write and 'phone in comments about the music played on the radio. Many disc-jockeys run dances, promote shows, work as DJs in bars and clubs and as MCs introducing a variety of acts. Ray Henderson of WCHB, for example, has worked as an MC with Otis Redding, James Brown and Joe Tex. Pervis Spann and E. Rodney Jones of WVON promote blues and soul music concerts in Chicago. Were they unable to reflect and anticipate the

GEE   HAL ATKINS   GREGORY   FRANKIE CROCKER   JEFFREY TROY   JERRY B.

the SOUL brothers

NEW SOUNDS

Number	Judy Clay & William Bell	Land Of Love	The Moon Peop
From Maria	Joe Simon	Breakin' Your Promise	The Delfon
ance Your Love	The Five Stairsteps & Cubie	There Was A Time	Gene Chand
Jack	Andre Williams	Who Is Gonna Love Me	Dionne Warw
ve Her All The Love I Got	Benny Gordon	You Got What I Need	Freddie Sc
reen Apples	O. C. Smith	Emavungwini	Miriam Mak
itty	Riccardo Ray	I Worry About You	Irene R
	Jay Lewis	I Won't Do Anything	Lezli Valent
That	Tina Britt	Funky Judge	Bull & The Matad
mmers	Ray Barretto	I Can't Dance To That Music	Martha Reeves & The Vandel
alley P.T.A.	Bobbi Martin	Fly Me To The Moon	Bobby Woma
		Unchained Melody	The Sweet Inspirati
		Standing On The Outside	Brenda Jo Har

BOSS BLUES

		Help Yourself	James & Bobby Pur
		She's About A Mover	Otis C
		Keep That Man	Big Maybe
		That's In The Past	Brenda & The Tabulati
ned Her That Way	James Carr	You're The Lovliest Song I Ever Heard	Johnnie &
e Away	Toussaint McCall	Do What You Gotta Do	Nina Sim
ible You	Billy Harner	Cupid	Ricky Le

tastes of their audience they would soon be out of business. Thirdly, some disc-jockeys are singers and musicians themselves. Both E. Rodney Jones (WVON) and Enoch Gregory (WWRL) have made records. Fourthly, all the programme directors and disc-jockeys in this study are black and have in general shared the same musical socialisation as their audiences. Finally, their statements about black music echo conversations the author has had with black Americans during a period of four years.

The proportion of blues played on black radio is small. Programme directors and disc-jockeys are unanimous in stating that over the past ten or 15 years this proportion has grown smaller and smaller. They predict the trend will continue. They receive fewer blues in promotion copies from record companies; there are fewer blues in the returns from record shops showing their best-selling records. Evidence from discographies supports these observations. Figure 1, based on data from Leadbitter and Slaven's *Blues Records: 1943-1966*, illustrates the decreasing number of blues records released. Since we are concerned solely with the black market, only singles (78s and 45s) have been included, as they form the vast majority of blues records purchased by that market. Most companies producing blues for a black audience issue only a handful of long-playing records. Few LPs by blues artists are found in ghetto record shops. The

WVON SOUL FORTY-FIVE LIST
JULY 12,-----JULY 18,1968

	TITLE	ARTIST
1.	GRAZING IN THE GRASS	HUGH MASEKELA
2.	STONE SOUL PICNIC	5th DIMENSION
3.	NEVER GIVE YOU UP	JERRY BUTLER
4.	THE HORSE	CLIFF NOBLES
5. A.	HERE COMES THE JUDGE	SHORTY LONG
5. B.	HERE COMES THE JUDGE	PIGMEAT MARKHAM
6.	SLIP AWAY	CLARANCE CARTER
7.	HERE I AM BABY	MARVALETTES
8. A.	YESTERLOVE	MIRACLES
8. B.	MUCH BETTER OFF	MIRACLES
9.	WORKIN' ON A GROOVY THING	PATTI DREW
10.	LOVE MAKES A WOMAN	BARBARA ACKLIN
11.	YOU'RE LOSING ME	BARBARA LYNN
12.	I'M A MIDNIGHT MOVER	WILSON PICKETT
13. A.	THINK	ARETHA FRANKLIN
13. B.	YOU SEND ME	ARETHA FRANKLIN
14.	STAY IN MY CORNER	DELLS
15.	LISTEN HERE	EDDIE HARRIS
16.	LOOK OVER YOUR SHOULDER	O'JAYS
17.	PEOPLE SURE ACT FUNNY	ARTHUR CONLEY
18.	SAVE YOUR LOVE FOR ME	BOBBY BLAND
19.	I NEVER FOUND ME A GIRL	EDDIE FLOYD
20.	YOU'RE TUFF ENOUGH	JUNIOR WELLS
21.	I'M GETTIN' LONG ALRIGHT	RAELETTES
22. A.	ELINOR RIGBY	RAY CHARLES
22. B.	UNDERSTANDING	RAY CHARLES
23.	THE LOVE I FOUND IN YOU	BROS. OF SOUL
24.	YOU MET YOUR MATCH	STEVIE WONDER
25.	DARK END OF THE STREET	LITTLE MILTON
26. A.	THE WOMAN I LOVE	B.B. KING
26. B.	WHAT THEY DO TO ME	B.B. KING
27.	SWEETEST FEELING	JACKIE WILSON
28.	BASEBALL GAME	INTRUDERS
29.	SEND MY BABY BACK	FREDDIE HUGHES
30.	GOD BLESS OUR LOVE	BALLADS
31.	I KNOW I CAN	ESQUIRES
32.	I'M HIP TO YOUR GAME	RENALDO DOMINO
33.	TELL ME THE TRUTH	BILLY STEWART
34.	I CAN'T STOP DANCING	ARCHIE & DRELLS
35.	SOUL MEETING	SOUL CLAN
36.	HARD TO HANDLE	OTIS REDDING
37.	THE FUNKY JUDGE	BULL & MATADORS
38.	DON'T LET HIM TAKE YOUR LOVE	JIMMY RUFFIN
39.	FOR GIRLS TO BE LONELY	BOBBY MARCHAN
40.	LEAN ON ME	TONY FOX
41.	BROADWAY FREEZE	HARVEY SCALES
42.	I AM YOUR MAN	BOBBY TAYLOR
43.	THE LOVE I NEED	RUBY ANDREWS
44. A.	LIGHT MY FIRE	JOSE FELICIANO
44. B.	CALIFORNIA DREAMIN'	JOSE FELICIANO
45.	PLEASE RETURN YOUR LOVE TO ME	TEMPTATIONS
PICK:	YOU'RE ALL I NEED TO GET BY	MARVIN & TAMMI
TOO HOT:	WITHOUT YOUR LOVE	JOHNNY MOORE

ED COOK
"NASSAU DADDY"

BERNADINE C. WASHINGTON

HERB KENT
"THE KOOL GENT"

E. RODNEY JONES
"THE MAD LAD"

WESLEY SOUTH

LUCKY CORDELL

JOE COBB
"YOUNG BLOOD"

PERVIS SPANN
"THE BLUES MAN"

ROY WOOD

JIM MALONEY

FRANKLIN McCARTHY
"SUGAR DADDY"

Don Cornelius

CLAIR NELSON

BILL "DOC" LEE

majority of postwar blues LPs are issued by such companies as Vanguard, Folkways, Arhoolie and Testament for a largely white market. Many are of traditional country blues which no longer sell in the black market. Records on these labels are seldom if ever found in ghetto record shops or played on black radio. Companies specialising in the white market rarely issue singles.

From 1943 to 1947 there is a steady increase in the number of blues

KUXL RADIO/1570

1. BABY BABY DON'T CRY Smokey Robinson & the Miracles
2. GIVE IT UP & TURN IT LOOSE James Brown
3. EVERY DAY PEOPLE-Sly & the Family Stones
4. THERE'S GONNA BE A SHOWDOWN-Archie Bell & the Drells.
5. CAN I CHANGE MY MIND-Tyrone Davis
6. I FORGOT TO BE YOUR LOVER-William Bell
7. GOOD LOVING AIN'T EASY TO COME BY-Marvin Gaye & Tammi Terrell
8. I'M GONNA MAKE YOU LOVE ME-Diana Ross,The Supremes & Temptations
9. RIOT-Hugh Maskala
10. TAKE CARE OF YOUR HOMEWORK-Johnny Taylor
11. BEGINNING OF MY END-Unifics
12. I STOLE SOME LOVE-Don Convay & Goodtimers
13. HEY JUDE-Wilson Pickett
14. MELINDA-Bobby Taylor & Vancouvers
15. SOCK A POO POO-69 Part II Maurice McKinnes & the Champions
16. SOUL SISTER BROWN SUGAR-Sam & Dave
17. LOOKING BACK-Joe Simon
18. GETTING THE CORNERS-The Toronadoes
19. LIVING IN SHAME-Diana Ross & the Supremes
20. SQUEEZE-Dynamic 7
21. HOMECOOKING-Jr.Walker & the All Stars
22. 30-60-90-Willie Mitchell
23. THIS OLD HEART OF MINE-Tammi Terrell
24. THE WEIGHT-Aretha Franklin
25. MY WORLD ENDED THE DAY YOU LEFT ME-David Ruffin
26. GIVE HER A TRANSPLANT-Intruders
27. DON'T DESTROY ME-Marale Hendrix
28. TILL I CAN'T TAKE IT ANYMORE-Ben E.King
29. TWENTY FIVE MILES-Edwin Starr
30. OILY-Juggy

THE BEST OF SAM & DAVE
Atlantic SD 8218

    PICK HIT

COAL MAN-Mick Rice

LAST WEEKS PICK HIT
THERE'LL COME A TIME-Betty Everett

KUXL'S HOT KICKER......
CLOUD NINE-Mongo Santamaria

LAST WEEKS HOT KICKER
SNATCHING IT BACK-Clarence Carter

    NEW RECORDS
1. I'VE GOT TO HAVE YOUR LOVE-Eddie Floyd
2. I DON'T KNOW WHY-Stevie Wonder
3. FOOLISH FOOL-Dee Dee Warwick
4. BABY MAKE ME FEEL SO GOOD-Five Stairsteps
5. WHEN HE TOUCHES ME-Peaches & Herb
6. WHO'S MAKING LOVE-Youngholt Unlimited

TOO HOT TO HOLD
I TAKE CARE OF HOMEWORK-Syl Johnson

LAST WEEKS TOO HOT TO HOLD
MY WHOLE WORLD ENDED-David Ruffin

J A C K H A R R I S

KUXL'S DADDY SOUL

PRESENTS

TOP SOUL THIRTY

recordings from the lowest to the highest number in the years included in the sample. The major decline in the number of releases begins after 1954. Three factors explain the dearth of blues during and immediately following World War II. Firstly, there was a government restriction, beginning in 1942, on the number of records released, due to the wartime demand for shellac. Secondly, in July 1942, The American Federation of Musicians banned all commercial recording for two years, fearing that juke boxes would reduce the demand for live music (Dixon and Godrich 1970: 99). Thirdly, many of the large companies with national distribution networks, which had formerly issued 'race records', discontinued this policy immediately or shortly after the war. It took some time before small independent companies began operations and fully met the demand for blues records. The decline in the popularity of blues after 1954 forms the subject of this book.

Date of recording	Number of records issued	BLUES RECORDS 1943 – 1966
1943	10	
1944	50	
1945	120	
1946	160	
1947	280	
1948	170	
1949	320	
1950	270	
1951	310	
1952	270	
1953	220	
1954	230	
1955	150	
1956	120	
1957	160	
1958	100	
1959	110	
1960	140	
1961	140	
1962	110	
1963	70	
1964	80	
1965	80	
1966	90	

Figure 1.

All blues singles (78s and 45s) listed in Leadbitter and Slaven's discography Blues Records 1943-1966 *are included in the table. Date of recording rather than date of release is given. Where the recording date covers more than one year, e.g. 1944-6, records are divided equally between those years. Unissued recordings are not included. Recordings that are released are included. Totals are rounded to the nearest ten.*

Nostalgia and Blues: Getting Back To It All

Turning to live performances of blues in Chicago and Detroit, a strong minority support for particular artists may be found, despite the general disinterest in the music. A blues concert on 3 and 4 August 1968 at the Regal Theatre, 47th and South Parkway, on Chicago's South Side, played to five capacity or near-capacity audiences. The show featured B.B. King,

Albert King, Junior Parker, Bobby Bland and Little Milton. In Detroit, Bobby Bland's advertised appearance (he failed to make the venue) at Prince Hall, Gratiot and McDougall, 22 July 1968, brought a full house. Yet even where blues finds support, there is evidence of a recognition by audiences and performers alike that the music is something of an anachronism. The show at the Regal is scattered with references to the past and to the South and with suggestions that blues is removed in time and space from its origins and heyday.

Little Milton introduces a slow blues with the words 'Time to go to school y'all. Here we go!' and when interviewed, explains, 'This is the beginning, this is from way back.' A standard part of B.B. King's act is a medley of old blues songs which he prefaces with 'Now we're gonna go way, way back.' Before several numbers he shouts to the audience, 'If you remember it, let me hear it,' which draws applause and shouts of 'yeah' after the first line of the song. B.B. King's act has changed little over the years. His 1968 appearance at the Regal is almost identical to his LP 'Live at the Regal' recorded in 1964. Rereleases of his earlier recordings sometimes sell as well as his current releases. The WVON top 45 records for Chicago dated 18 July 1968 has King's *The Woman I Love*, a rerelease of his 1959 recording, placed at equal 26 with his current hit *I'm Gonna Do What They Do To Me*. Talking about his audience Junior Parker states, 'The people expect me to do the tunes they remember. We always have to do the old standards like *Five Long Years, Driving Wheel* and *Next Time You See Me*. They really go for these.' He adds that his audience demands he retain his past image and recreate his past music in the style in which it was first performed. Talking about his harmonica-playing, which is featured in many of his earlier songs, but dropped from his later recordings, Junior Parker says 'I hate to play 'em, I really hate to play 'em. But this is part of the thing that identifies me. My audience loves me for playin' it so I have to play it.' Bobby Bland also sticks closely to well-tried standards. He regularly includes in his act such traditional and oft-recorded songs as *St. James Infirmary, Stormy Monday* and *Drifting Blues*, with his early hits such as *The Feeling Is Gone* and *Turn On Your Lovelight*. Their arrangement and performance differs little from the original recordings of the '50s and early '60s. All singers feature their latest release, Bobby Bland's being *Save Your Love For Me*, which he describes as 'an old blues ballad of twenty years ago.' Albert King too feels the pressure of the conservative blues audience, and suggests he is held back as an artist by the demand for old traditional blues. He states simply, 'I don't like playin' this old time stuff.'

As well as being removed in time from today, performers and audience recognise that blues is somewhat removed in place from Chicago. Introducing *Five Long Years,* Junior Parker says, 'Alright, we're gonna put you there. Everybody got the blues tonight. We're gonna take you straight back to Jackson, Mississippi.' He acknowledges the Southern 'downhome'

origins of his audience by beginning his performance on 3 August with
'Everybody from Tennessee, Arkansas and Mississippi say yeah!' and is
greeted with an affirmative roar. The following evening he shouts,
'Everybody from Alabama and Mississippi say yeah!' which produces a
similar response. Albert King takes his audience back home as he
introduces *Wrapped Up In Love Again* with 'Yeah, we're goin' on down
behind the sun,' a reference to the Deep South.

In historical terms performances suggest that blues is set in the past, in
geographical terms they imply it is set in the South. Neither performances
in general nor the music in particular have changed much over the past ten
years. Audiences are conservative, preferring old songs and old arrangements.

The fact that shows such as the blues concert at the Regal are well
attended, but blues in general is rarely played on black radio or recorded
for a black audience, raises an interesting paradox. It may be resolved by
suggesting that nostalgia is an important function of the present-day
performance of blues in the North. This suggestion has the merit of
explaining both the paucity of blues on radio and record and the high
attendance at live performances. For nostalgia to be effectively evoked,
the stimulus must be infrequent. If scenes from the past are continually
resurrected, if old memories are revived daily, the process ceases to be

Left: *B.B. King.* Above: *Bobby Bland.*

emotionally stimulating. If nostalgia is an important element in blues today, a radio station with a blues format would not meet this need, but an occasional visit to a blues concert would. This is the situation that exists and the interpretation put forward here appears to explain it. It further suggests that black audiences at blues concerts don't want to be continuously assailed with the music because it no longer forms a part of their daily lives. Blues is no longer an integral part of the present. At least in the North, a blues show appears to be as much a means of getting back to it all as a means of getting away from it all.

Blues and Blues: Modern and Downhome

Despite this emphasis on the past, only certain blues singers within a particular style attract large black audiences. According to promoters in Chicago, B.B. King, Bobby Bland, Junior Parker, Albert King and Little Milton (the big five), whose styles are considered modern, are the biggest draws, whereas artists such as Howling Wolf, Muddy Waters and John Lee Hooker, seen as more traditional and old-fashioned singers, could never hope to fill a large theatre. B.B. King and the others at the Regal played to capacity or near-capacity houses. But Muddy Waters' well advertised appearance on a Saturday night at the Cozy Bar in the Minneapolis North Side ghetto drew an audience which was no larger than the usual turnout for the regularly featured local soul band, unknown outside Minneapolis. However, Junior Parker's appearance at the same venue attracted considerably larger crowds. John Lee Hooker, in Detroit for a couple of weeks in the summer of 1968 to appear at a rally in support of Senator Eugene McCarthy's bid for the Presidency, appeared only once at a black venue, the Rapa House, during his stay. Although the Rapa House is hardly a suitable place for a large blues audience—a coffee house run by blacks and patronised mainly by a theatrical and show business crowd—Hooker's appearance, despite advertising in the black press, drew fewer than 20 blacks. The different drawing power of modern and traditional blues applies also to their performance by lesser known, locally based singers. Alex Cramer after a visit to Chicago in 1971 noted that Mighty Joe Young is one of the most successful local blues singers. 'He plays a very modern style of blues similar to B.B. King ... Because Young plays contemporary blues things are relatively good for him.' However, singers such as Hound Dog Taylor and J.B. Hutto, whose styles are more traditional and akin to those of Muddy Waters and Elmore James, are not very successful, averaging a meagre fifteen dollars a booking. (Cramer 1971: 5)

Singers such as Muddy Waters, Howling Wolf, John Lee Hooker and Lightnin' Hopkins are often bracketed together and their style described variously as 'gutbucket', 'lowdown', 'dirty', 'down in the alley', 'down-home' and more recently 'funky blues'. The associations of these terms are often pejorative and the style they describe is seen as old-fashioned. The style of the big five, with the occasional exception of Albert King, is referred to as 'modern' or 'clean'. The differences between 'dirty' and 'clean' blues and the reasons for these epithets will be discussed later in this chapter.

Further evidence for the greater popularity of modern blues comes from record shops, juke boxes and radio stations. The big five are always represented in ghetto record shops, usually by several singles, including their current release. The odd downhome records are in evidence, but not nearly in such numbers as modern blues. Owners of record shops typically state 'They just don't sell.' Similarly, most juke boxes in black bars and clubs feature the latest B.B. King single and sometimes records by Bobby Bland and other modern singers. Visits to scores of black bars revealed only one downhome blues on a juke-box—*It Was Early One Morning* by Mojo Buford—at the Regal Tavern, Minneapolis, where Mojo and his band played regularly. Most new releases by the big five are played on black radio stations and some feature in the charts they compile, but downhome records are rarely played. Blues records by artists other than the big five are usually played at the wish and discretion of the disc-jockey rather than as the policy of the station, or as a reflection of what is selling to the black public. Ed Cook, an older disc-jockey at WVON, plays the odd record by Charles Brown and Jimmy McCracklin. Jack Harris (KUXL) plays an occasional Lowell Fulsom release. But again these records are nearer modern than downhome blues. Martha Jean of WJLB, Detroit, provides the main exception in the radio stations surveyed for this study. She sometimes plays downhome blues, and is particularly partial to Muddy Waters. It is important to note that even in Chicago, which fostered the maturity and success of Muddy Waters and Howling Wolf and many other downhome singers, modern blues are far more popular. This becomes particularly apparent from the fact that these two singers and similar artists record for Chess Records, owned by the Chess brothers who also own WVON, Chicago's largest black radio station. One would expect these singers to get at least moderate airplay on WVON, as indeed they have in the past. With the exception of Little Milton, a modern blues singer who recorded for Chess (on the Checker label), downhome blues singers on Chess receive the same treatment on WVON as on other radio stations.

Memphis and Modern Blues

To appreciate the differing popularity of modern blues and downhome blues, it is necessary to explore their evolution. Exemplified by Memphis blues and Chicago blues, both styles developed contemporaneously. Modern blues, as represented by the music of the big five, evolved in Memphis in the late '40s and early '50s. B.B. King cut his first record in 1949, Bobby Bland in 1950, Junior Parker in 1952 and Little Milton in 1953. All cut their early records and developed their styles in Memphis. Albert King made a lone record in 1953, but he only began recording regularly in 1959 in St Louis and later (1966) in Memphis.

It is clear from their accounts of their careers that these singers shared important influences which included each other. Together they created what Charles Keil has termed the 'Memphis synthesis'. B.B. King, born at 'a little place between Itta Bena and Indianola in Mississippi', grew up listening to country blues. He recalls,

> As a kid I listened to people like Blind Lemon, Blind Boy Fuller and my cousin Bukka White, Bumble Bee Slim, Peetie Wheatstraw and Lonnie Johnson, all these people I liked as a kid. My ma would buy a lot of records, and usually these were by artists that were popular among the country people, especially in the Delta.

B.B. names T-Bone Walker as a later but important influence on his style. Bobby Bland also remembers growing up with country blues.

> The old country blues were all around me in the environment I grew up in. I was born in a little place that's not really on the map, they call it Rosemark, Tennessee; it's right out from Memphis. Blind

Lemon and Memphis Minnie, this was the kind of music my parents dug.

Discussing his later influences Bobby Bland states, 'I used to sing exactly like B.B. because this was my idol along with T-Bone Walker, Lowell Fulsom, Jimmy Witherspoon and Johnny Ace.' Little Milton grew up as 'a country boy lovin' the blues' in Inverness, Mississippi. His earliest influences were Sonny Boy Williamson (Rice Miller), Willie Love and Joe Willie Wilkins, and later,

> when my career got started I was inspired by a lot of cats but some of the people I really idolise were Roy Brown, Joe Turner, and B.B. who was a big name even then, and T-Bone Walker.

Junior Parker, born in West Memphis, Arkansas, gives Sonny Boy Williamson as a major influence.

> My greatest idol was Mr. Sonny Boy Williamson. Back in 1948 I played my first professional job with his band playing harmonica. He'd play and I'd play. That's where I got the name Junior from because everybody thought I was his son. Back in the forties, I really used to try and sound like Roy Brown.

Albert King, born and raised in Indianola, Mississippi, recalls his old-time favourite Peetie Wheatstraw and gives Lonnie Johnson and T-Bone Walker as important figures in the development of his style.

The big five grew up in the Delta states of Mississippi, Arkansas and Tennessee. They were all influenced by the country blues style of that area, and its later development in the person of singers like Sonny Boy Williamson. They were also influenced by the Texas urban blues style founded largely by T-Bone Walker and developed by singers such as Roy Brown. A lesser influence can be detected, the jazz blues of the Kansas City tradition, in the persons of Jimmy Witherspoon and Joe Turner. These three styles, Delta country blues, Texas urban blues, and Kansas City jazz blues, were brought together in Memphis and a new style emerged.

Turning to the guitar styles of B.B. King, Albert King and Little Milton, a similar synthesis is apparent. All three began by accompanying themselves on guitar in country blues style, playing both bass and treble parts. They later formed bands and played single string runs. B.B. King and Albert King both give T-Bone Walker and Lonnie Johnson as primary influences on their guitar styles. B.B. King compares his early style to Lonnie Johnson's: 'He had a somewhat like modern style–that is comparing to the stuff that I was playin' and a lot of other people were playin'. He had a modern technique of chord progressions' (*Soul Sounds* 31 October 1968: 5). Little Milton, who lists T-Bone Walker and B.B. King

Left: *Albert King.*

as formative influences on his own guitar style, discusses the 'clean' style of blues guitar,

> T-Bone, now there's a cat. T-Bone Walker inspired me and a lot more guitar players and singers because that cat always played clean. He would like pick one string at a time and most of the other guitar players in those days man would like frail it and make chords. He played one string at a time, no sweats. Then B.B. King came along. I'm sure he got a lot of pointers from T-Bone Walker.

Wayne Bennett, recently retired as guitarist in Joe Scott's band which accompanied Bobby Bland on tour and on record, plays in the style which emerged from the Memphis synthesis. Beginning with a foundation of Delta country blues guitar techniques, B.B. King, Little Milton and Albert King added the more jazz-influenced styles of T-Bone Walker and Lonnie Johnson and developed the Memphis guitar style.

In the late '40s and early '50s, B.B. King, Bobby Bland, Junior Parker and Little Milton were based in Memphis and their mutual influence may be surmised from their activities. In 1949 B.B. King formed a small band, the Beale Streeters, which included Johnny Ace on piano, and in 1950 Bobby Bland was added as a featured singer. Bobby Bland notes he began by sounding exactly like B.B. King, and attributes much of his later blues ballad style to Johnny Ace. As well as performing together, the Beale Streeters played on each other's records. Johnny Ace later led his own revue which included Bobby Bland and was joined in 1953 by Junior Parker. After Johnny Ace's death—he killed himself playing Russian roulette backstage at a Houston theatre, on Christmas Eve 1954—Bobby Bland and Junior Parker jointly led the revue. Little Milton, who began his career slightly later, had the fame of his predecessors to contend with. He recalls,

> I got my career half way moving and I had people come up and it kind of bugged me at the beginning. They would say, 'You sound like T-Bone Walker, you sound like Roy Brown, you sound just like B.B. King.' Then comes Bobby Bland, we like been good friends for a number of years and now they started saying, 'You sound like Bobby Bland, you sound like all of them.'

Sharing the same early influences, Memphis singers also influenced each other.

As we have noted, the two major ingredients of the Memphis synthesis were Delta blues and Texas urban blues. Firstly, why the strong component of Delta country blues? Country blues, as their name suggests, find their main support in rural areas. The isolation of rural blacks in the Delta and particularly in Mississippi probably maintained the tradition of country blues there longer than elsewhere. Mississippi has no large urban centres, like Houston or Dallas in Texas, which by their nature are a context for change. Next, blacks from the Delta usually migrate northwards, and Memphis, on the northern edge of the Delta, is the first major urban centre on that route. Howling Wolf and John Lee Hooker, both born in Mississippi, spent several years in Memphis, before going north to Chicago (Wolf) and Cincinnati then Detroit (Hooker). Born in Mississippi or in and around Memphis, B.B. King, Little Milton, Junior Parker and Bobby Bland, like their audiences, brought a strong tradition of Delta blues to Memphis.

Why was post-war Texas, or more correctly Texas-West Coast, urban blues the other main component of the Memphis synthesis? Firstly, this style, exemplified by T-Bone Walker, Amos Milburn, Roy Brown, Clarence 'Gatemouth' Brown and Charles Brown, preceded the Memphis synthesis by a few years and so provided a ready-made model for the latter. T-Bone Walker, born in Linden, Texas, began recording in 1940 (apart from an early recording in 1929) and made most of his records in Los Angeles and Hollywood. Amos Milburn, born in Houston, Texas, began recording in Los Angeles in 1945. Clarence 'Gatemouth' Brown, born in Vinton, Louisiana, began recording in Los Angeles in 1947 and from 1949 onwards recorded in Houston. Compared with the Memphis synthesis, Texas-West Coast blues were relatively unaffected by Delta blues. Texas had its own blues tradition, and black Texans usually migrate west to Oakland and Los Angeles rather than to Memphis and the North. A style that had developed largely from its own precedents was thus provided as a model for the Memphis synthesis. Secondly, blacks living in urban centres in the Delta such as Memphis and Helena, Arkansas, could hear Texas blues on radio programmes. B.B. King worked for three and a half years as a disc-jockey at WDIA in Memphis, the first radio station programmed entirely for a black audience. Thirdly, Texas-West Coast blues were an urban development and therefore suited to a city like Memphis. Country blues with lyrics about floods and picking cotton and references to mules and 'poor country boys' were closely associated with rural life. The city with a substantially different way of life demanded a new form of music. The linking of Texas-West Coast urban blues with Delta country blues reflected this change of life-style and setting, and the Memphis synthesis emerged as urban blues. With the change in music, the more obvious references to rural life were dropped from the lyrics.

Chicago Downhome Blues

The evolution of 'modern' Memphis blues was paralleled in time by the development of a further blues style, Chicago 'downhome' blues. Of all the postwar styles, Chicago has the closest links with the country blues of the Delta. As with Memphis, its exponents were drawn from the Delta and the style evolved in the late '40s and '50s. The following singers exemplify the Chicago style and their states of origin and the dates when they first began to record in Chicago are given: Muddy Waters–Mississippi, 1947: Little

Walter–Louisiana, 1947: Robert Nighthawk–Arkansas, 1948: Johnny Shines–Tennessee (Memphis), 1950; J.B. Lenoir–Mississippi, 1952; Junior Wells–Arkansas (West Memphis), 1953; Howling Wolf–Mississippi, 1953; Elmore James–Mississippi, 1953; Willie Nix–Tennessee (Memphis), 1953; Walter Horton–Mississippi, 1954; Sonny Boy Williamson, Mississippi, 1955. Like the leading figures in the Memphis synthesis, the Chicago singers were born either in the Delta states or in Memphis on the northern edge of the Delta. Again like their 'modern' blues contemporaries, the Chicago 'downhome' bluesmen played together in public and on each other's records. Their mutual influence and the compatibility of their styles can be surmised from a couple of examples; Muddy Waters played on records by Little Walter, Junior Wells and Sonny Boy Williamson; Walter Horton accompanied Johnny Shines and Muddy Waters on record; Junior Wells appears on records by J.B. Lenoir.

The Chicago style also developed in Memphis and the Delta. Elmore James made his first records accompanied by Sonny Boy Williamson in Jackson, Mississippi, in 1952, and spent some time in Willie Nix's band in Memphis. Thereafter he alternated mainly between Chicago and the Delta. Howling Wolf first recorded in Memphis in 1948, where he had some success as a singer and DJ before moving to Chicago in 1952. Sonny Boy Williamson was also popular in Memphis and the Delta as a singer and disc-jockey. He recorded in Jackson, Mississippi, before going north. Both Willie Nix and Walter Horton recorded and performed in Memphis before going to Chicago. Most of the other Chicago 'downhome' singers made their first records in that city. We may suggest that one of the reasons why these singers moved to or worked in Chicago was because there was a greater demand for their style of blues there than in Memphis. Howling Wolf's early sides recorded in Memphis had been leased to Chess Records in Chicago and sold well enough for that company to buy his contract from RPM in the early '50s. About the same time Chess bought Sonny Boy Williamson's contract from Trumpet Records of Jackson, Mississippi. As the Memphis synthesis developed, the popularity of 'downhome' blues in that city may well have declined.

Tracing the development of Chicago blues we find a direct evolution from the country styles of the Delta. Whereas Memphis is a synthesis of styles, Chicago represents a development of one major style. Unlike 'modern' Memphis singers, Chicago bluesmen normally give only country blues singers or each other as their major influences. Muddy Waters lists Son House and Robert Johnson, Johnny Shines names Robert Johnson, Elmore James also gives Robert Johnson and adds Kokomo Arnold, Howling Wolf gives Charlie Patton and Little Walter names Sonny Boy Williamson. The influence of Delta singers may be found in a relatively uncontaminated form in the recordings of Chicago bluesmen. Taking Robert Johnson as an example, we may trace his influence on Chicago blues. Johnny Shines's *Ramblin'* is based on Robert Johnson's *Ramblin'*

On My Mind and his *Dynaflow Blues* is a remake of Johnson's *Terraplane Blues*, with similar lyrics and a close copy of Johnson's guitar accompaniment. Elmore James's oft-recorded theme song *Dust My Broom* is based on Robert Johnson's *I Believe I'll Dust My Broom*. One of the first songs Muddy Waters learned was Johnson's *Walking Blues*, which forms the basis of Muddy's *I Feel Like Going Home*. Turning to guitar styles, Muddy Waters, Robert Nighthawk, Elmore James, J.B. Lenoir, Johnny Shines, J.B. Hutto and other Chicago bluesmen continued and developed the Delta bottleneck guitar style epitomised by Son House and Robert Johnson.

The Chicago style has often been described as amplified or electrified country blues. Country blues, often performed by a singer accompanying himself on accoustic guitar, are transposed into the context of a small group, usually consisting of electric guitar, bass, drums, harmonica and sometimes piano. This process in itself inevitably changes the music, as Homesick James, a Chicago-based singer, explains as he discusses his recording of *Crossroads,* based on Robert Johnson's *Standing At The Crossroads*. Using Johnson's words but the arrangement from his cousin Elmore James's recording of the song, Homesick notes,

> Well I can play the Johnson way, the way I learned from the record, but I generally just do it myself. I suppose it would be possible to do it with a modern band, but since the changes are so irregular, the other musicians would have to be familiar with the way Robert Johnson played it. Then they could follow me. (Napier and Leadbitter 1965: 8)

A group brought a certain standardisation to the country blues. Backed by several musicians a singer could not change chords or alter the arrangement at will. Despite these differences, Chicago downhome blues is unmistakeably the country blues come to town. The style is an evolution, not a synthesis.

Why did Chicago blues develop in the late '40s and in the '50s? Why is the style based on Delta precedents? These questions can in part be answered together. The vast migration of blacks from the South reached its peak in the decade 1940-50 and has continued, at a slightly reduced level, to the present—see Figure 2.

Figure 2

Time Period	Net black out-migration from the South
1910–1920	450,000
1920–1930	750,000
1930–1940	350,000
1940–1950	1,600,000
1950–1960	1,460,000
1960–1970	1,400,000

Figures rounded to the nearest 10,000

(Adapted from National Advisory Commission 1968: 240)

Slowed by the Depression years, this migration was accelerated by the demands of wartime industry for large numbers of unskilled workers for the Northern factories. The Korean War continued the demands of World War II for labour though at a somewhat reduced level. The pull from the North was compounded by a push from the South due to the increasing mechanisation of farming, particularly in the cultivation and harvesting of cotton. Tractors, mechanical cotton pickers and chemical weed killers pushed many black farmworkers off the land. An impression of the scale of the migration comes from the observations of a black porter who has travelled for over 32 years on the Illinois Central Railroad which runs from New Orleans through the Mississippi Delta to Chicago.

> It started in 1947. This train went through the Delta, and there was nothing but black faces for years, and years, and years. I used to wonder, 'Where are they coming from? How can there be anybody left? My God, they must be coming right out of the ground. They got to stop sometime.' Well, a couple of years ago, it seemed to slack off. You begin to see some whites now. Used to be twenty-thirty Negroes for every white on this train. Now its more like three-to-one. (Bagdikian 1967: 66)

Turning in particular to Chicago in the North and Mississippi and the Delta states in the South, we find an important relationship. From 1955-60 almost 60% of non-white migrants to Chicago came from Mississippi, Tennessee, Arkansas, Louisiana and Alabama, migrants from Mississippi making up nearly one-third of this figure (National Advisory Commission 1968: 240). (The category 'non-white' includes 92% black Americans on a national basis. This percentage is subject to regional variation.) From 1950-60, 323,000 blacks migrated from Mississippi alone, more than from any other state (Oliver 1965: 13). Chicago's black population from 1940-60 increased by over 200%, rising to 890,000, 24% of the city's population (Taeuber and Taeuber 1966: 311). Many of the migrants came from rural areas. Throughout this century Mississippi has had both the largest number of black farm workers and the largest number leaving the land. Figure 3 shows this process.

Figure 3
Black farm operators in the United States, 1930–1959

State	1959	1950	1940	1930
North Carolina	41,000	69,000	57,000	75,000
Tennessee	15,000	24,000	28,000	35,000
Alabama	29,000	57,000	73,000	94,000
Mississippi	55,000	123,000	159,000	183,000
Arkansas	15,000	41,000	57,000	80,000
Louisiana	18,000	41,000	60,000	74,000
Texas	15,000	34,000	53,000	86,000

Figures rounded to the nearest 10,000

(Adapted from Beale 1966: 171)

Most black Chicago migrants came from the Delta and were rural farm workers. As such they were the most isolated and traditional section of black America and had the greatest commitment to Delta country blues. Their tastes in music were catered for by record companies such as Trumpet, which operated out of Jackson, Mississippi. Records produced by this company, which included sides by Elmore James and Sonny Boy Williamson, paralleled the style of Chicago blues. The migrants brought their musical tastes to Chicago and with them came the Delta blues singers.

The question of the development and popularity of Chicago downhome blues is not yet fully answered. Why did these migrants not develop the blues of the Memphis synthesis rather than the Chicago style? Firstly, many of them had probably never been exposed to Texas-West Coast urban blues and Kansas City jazz blues, the major ingredients along with Delta blues in the Memphis synthesis. Many lived beyond the range of radio broadcasts, which were beamed mainly to urban populations. The situation of many was probably little different from that described by Charles S. Johnson in the early '30s. In a study of isolated black communities in rural Alabama he noted that, in his sample of 612 families, 'There are no radios, but 76 families had victrolas . . .' (Johnson 1934; 184). Mojo Buford, born near Hernando, Mississippi, in 1929, recalls, 'We didn't have no radio, nothing out there in the country.' (*Blues Unlimited* 76: 13).

Locked in rural isolation, often without means of transport, black farmers lived in shacks in the middle of fields, serviced by unnamed dirt roads. In 1967, a 48-year-old sharecropper preparing to make the long journey north with his family states:

> I never been out of Mississippi except one time in my whole life, and that was only one week. Tell you the truth, up to the sixteenth day of March, 19 and 57, I never been out of Holmes County. (Bagdikian 1967: 27)

Like the way of life, blues changed little in the Delta.

Secondly, Chicago was a totally alien setting for rural migrants. They sought out the company of relatives and friends, and this process quickly built up village-like communities in an urban setting. There are two blocks in Chicago made up largely of Mississippians from Holmes County. Social life revolved round the folks from downhome as counties and small towns were contracted and re-formed on Chicago's South Side. Like most immigrant groups, black Chicagoans recreated, in a modified form, the institutions from back home. Store-front churches and blues bars and clubs sprang up as refuges from the strange and bewildering environment of a metropolitan city. The importance of these institutions was the creation of something familiar and therefore secure, giving life at least a

Right: *sharecropper cabins, Arkansas* (top) *and Mississippi.*

superficial continuity after the break in life-style, customs and climate. Unlike Chicago, Memphis, on the doorstep of the Delta, is not a long way from home, and the need to recreate the South there is not so great. Further, migration to Memphis was not on the same scale as that to Chicago. The vast and rapid exodus of blacks from the Delta to Chicago produced large numbers of people in the same situation, sufficiently large aggregates to recreate Mississippi in the 'Windy City'. In one sense Chicago downhome blues were an anachronism even as they were developing. In providing familiarity, continuity and security, they remained little changed from the traditional Delta blues upon which they were modelled.

Memphis and Chicago: 'Clean' and 'Dirty'

Returning to the present (1968), it is clear that in Chicago, as elsewhere, Memphis blues are far more popular than Chicago blues. Before suggesting reasons for this we shall first characterise Memphis blues using B.B. King as an example and Chicago blues as a point of reference. Starting from a Delta country blues base—he began by performing solo, accompanying himself on guitar—B.B. King added piano and drums and then saxes playing simple jazz-blues riffs. The latter are largely absent from Chicago blues. On amplified guitar, he played single string runs developed from T-Bone Walker and Lonnie Johnson. King's style is more melodic than T-Bone's, showing Lonnie Johnson's influence—Johnson is a particularly melodic guitarist. Both Lonnie Johnson and T-Bone Walker use ninth chords in their blues, a jazz influence, distinct from the majors and sevenths employed in country and Chicago blues. When B.B. King plays the occasional chord it is usually a ninth, and his guitar runs are played around a ninth chord, rather than playing minor notes against a major chord, a feature of Chicago blues. His guitar notes, usually played in the upper register, are clear and ringing, as opposed to the Chicago style which sometimes features a rough and even distorted guitar sound, and utilises bass notes to a greater degree. B.B. rarely uses his guitar as a percussive instrument, again in contrast with Chicago blues. Turning to his vocal style, in particular his timing, B.B. King sings more over and behind the beat than Chicago singers. Joe Scott, Bobby Bland's band leader, considers this technique a major factor in distinguishing the modern blues style. 'There's a strong beat blues where the words are right on the beat, and then you can do it the way "Spoon" [Jimmy Witherspoon] does it, taking your time, pausing and then catching up with the band' (Keil 1966: 62). When fans of B.B. King say he's 'more relaxed' and 'cool' than more traditional singers, they are probably responding in part to his timing. B.B. sings his songs, he never half-sings and half-talks as country and Chicago bluesmen sometimes do. He tends to use more melisma than these singers, a technique further developed by Bobby Bland. B.B. also makes use of vibrato in his singing, a feature which is particularly noticeable in some of

Junior Parker's songs. B.B. King's singing may be characterised as smoother, more fluid and more relaxed than Chicago blues. His fans make this comparison saying he 'sings smoother', 'sings sweeter' and he's 'more mellow'.

These characteristics are shared in varying degrees by Bobby Bland, Junior Parker and Little Milton. Bobby Bland sometimes incorporates techniques from gospel music into his songs. In *Yield Not To Temptation* he builds the song into a typical gospel climax with oft-repeated lines and a female chorus performing in the standard call-and-response pattern. Explaining his blues ballad style, using *Save Your Love For Me* as an example, Bobby states, 'I sing it pretty then go into the preacher stuff at the end.' Little Milton also incorporates gospel techniques into his songs and since the mid-'60s has developed steadily towards soul music. Albert King is on the fringe of the Memphis synthesis. His guitar follows somewhat the B.B. King pattern, but his vocal style and timing is more country blues based. A member of the Lamp Sisters responds to the old and the new in Albert's style. Watching him from the wings of the Regal Theatre, she remarks, 'How can he play so sweet and sing so dirty?'

As noted above, blues in the style of the Memphis synthesis are described as 'modern' and 'clean' in contrast to the 'dirty', 'gutbucket', 'lowdown' and 'downhome' blues of Chicago and the Delta. According to Little Milton, this distinction between blues styles began when B.B. King led the Memphis synthesis in the late '40s. 'When B.B. started coming up with his new thing, I think people were ready for a change. That's when they started calling the other kinds of blues gutbucket, they call it strictly down down.' When fans of B.B. King call Chicago and country blues 'dirty', or 'gutbucket', they often use the terms in a pejorative manner meaning crude, unsophisticated and unpolished. In part the terms used to describe the two forms of blues may be explained by the evolution of the music and the differences between the styles. Memphis blues are more 'modern' in temporal terms and certainly more cosmopolitan, utilising as they do various styles from different areas. Chicago blues are more closely tied to downhome in the Delta and retain a greater continuity with traditional styles. This is reflected in the term 'gutbucket', which also refers to the washtub bass used in traditional country blues bands. In terms of the overall sound of the two styles, it is possible from our characterisation to see why Memphis is regarded as 'smoother' and possibly therefore as 'cleaner'. However, we shall have to look further than the music to explain fully the more derogatory terms—'nasty', 'dirty' and 'alley music'—used to describe Chicago and Delta blues.

Music, like many other aspects of culture, is associated with particular groups of people. Black society is divided into rural and urban, into social classes, and into status and prestige groups. These divisions are defined by members of the society and a range of stereotypes characterising them accompanies the definitions. Distinctions in music in part refer to and are

B.B. King.

related to distinctions between social groups. The definition of social groups contains an evaluative element, the groups are ranked in terms of prestige. Similarly the distinctions within music have evaluative connotations. A study of black class structure reveals that the very terms used to classify and evaluate particular kinds of blues are used by upper and middle class blacks to describe and refer to lower class black society. These terms include 'dirty', 'nasty', 'unclean' and 'common alley niggers' (Davis, Gardner and Gardner 1965: Chapter 9). We may suggest that particular styles of blues are associated with particular classes and status groups within black society.

Urban blacks generally earned more money and regarded themselves as more sophisticated than their country cousins. The rural-urban dichotomy can be seen from a description by Son House of former sharecroppers returning to visit their rural friends in the Delta.

> At that time, there was mostly farm work, and sometimes it get pretty critical . . . Of course, they'd got plenty of just old common food, but they didn't make enough money to do any good . . . After they commenced waking up, some started going different places and come back with the news that they were doing so much better. 'Up in such and such a place, they pay so much and so much. That's what I make.' Well that wakes the other guys up. He sees his buddy all dressed up and looking so nice, and so they comment from one to the other and commence to easing out to these different places. (Charters 1967: 59)

With the new found wealth and status and the smart new clothes went the smart new blues. Memphis looked down on the Delta in more ways than one. The urban-rural dichotomy was symbolised by 'modern' Memphis blues and traditional Delta country blues.

In the '40s and '50s the newly arrived migrant in Chicago entered black society on the lowest rung of the social ladder. Often he arrived with little money, no job, no skills apart from farming and a rudimentary education. A Mississippi migrant expresses his situation before journeying north.

> I know in a city you's supposed to have an education. If you got me a job in the morning and I was supposed to separate the salt from the sugar, I couldn't do it, not if they was in the same kind of bag. I couldn't do it, cap'n, because I can't read. (Bagdikian 1967: 27)

As noted, the social frame of reference of many migrants was composed of people from 'downhome', and they brought the Delta blues north with them. Standardised negative stereotypes of newly arrived migrants are still found in Chicago; they are 'dirty' and they 'act ignorant' and 'talk funny'. These stereotypes are extended to 'downhome' Chicago blues, and the music is associated with social status.

Over page: *street corner, Chicago.*

Why has the blues style of the Memphis synthesis eclipsed Chicago blues even in Chicago itself? This is referable to a change in both the old migrants and the new. Migrants who had spent some time in Chicago became increasingly status-conscious and their aspirations widened in an urban context. Removed from the isolation of the Delta they were presented with many more standards of comparison and a more highly socially differentiated society. A perspective of survival was for many replaced by the conventional American dream. A Mississippi migrant family, after a few years in Chicago, states its hopes for the future:

> A better house with no rats, in a better neighbourhood, you know, some place for the kids to play in their own yard, with some grass in the back and in the front. (Bagdikian 1967: 67)

Modern Memphis blues were more in keeping with these perspectives than 'gutbucket' Chicago blues. Bobby Bland shows how Memphis blues relates to leaving behind the attitudes and lifestyle of the Delta: 'I still do the old blues like *Driftin' Blues* and *Stormy Monday* and I still sing them sadly, but I had to dress them up a bit to get in the better clubs because you had other types of people.' Bobby's smart, well-cut suits, careful grooming, immaculate 'process', his charm and good manners, and the relatively sophisticated arrangement and presentation of his music, were all in accord with the self-image and aspirations of many blacks in the '50s.

As migrants became oriented and established in an urban setting, they lost the need for hanging on to the past as a part of everyday life. The security and continuity provided by Chicago blues became less important. For many, blues became a nostalgic rather than an immediate experience. Again Memphis blues are more desirable for stimulating nostalgia without unwanted associations. Unlike Chicago's Delta-based blues, Keil states, Memphis blues, 'bring back memories of the "old country" without forcing their listeners to identify themselves as lower-class farmer types, or recent migrants from the South' (Keil 1966: 157).

A further factor leading to the decline of Chicago blues was a change in the nature of both the migration and the migrants. In the late '50s and early '60s both the rate and the direction of black migration changed. From 1960-3 the annual average of black migrants from the South was less than half that of 1940-50. Even more significantly, from 1960-3 there was a net black out-migration from the North-Central region, in which Chicago is the major city (Killingsworth 1969: 227). Changes were also taking place in the South. By 1960, 58% of Southern blacks lived in cities, and the majority of the rural population no longer worked on farms. While there were still around 60,000 black cotton pickers in the Delta in 1959, by 1967 their numbers had dwindled to 2,000 (*Newsweek* 24 July 1967: 23). More recent migrants to the North were as well educated as those already there (Taeuber 1969: 175-6). No longer were illiterate peasants descending in vast numbers upon Northern cities. The onrush of the Delta blues people to Chicago had slowed to a mere trickle.

The Old Folks from Down Home

Who buys blues records and goes to blues shows today? Firstly, older people. At the B.B. King concerts at the Regal, 80% of the audiences at two of the shows were estimated over 30 years of age and at least 50% over 40. Men and women were about equally represented. A similar pattern prevails at other blues shows with a rather higher proportion of young people at bars and clubs. Similarly, the small black market for blues records is made up largely of older people. Occasional observations include three men, ranging in age from their mid-40s to late 50s, who bought *The Woman I Love* by B.B. King, *Sittin' Here Thinkin'* by Lowell Fulsom and *That Did It* by Bobby Bland, and a woman of about 60 who bought *Back Door Friend* by Lightnin' Hopkins. Owners of ghetto record shops confirm these observations. A statement like 'It's the old folks from down home, they buy the blues' is typical.

As expected, those born and raised in Southern states provide the main following for blues in the North. Junior Parker's recognition of people from Alabama, Mississippi, Arkansas and Tennessee at the Regal reflects this. At a blues concert on Chicago's West Side, Charles Keil interviewed members of the audience and found that about one third was from

States of birth of blues singers who recorded from 1943 to 1966. Of all blues singers who recorded during these years, 30% are included. Compiled from data in Leadbitter & Slaven: 1968.

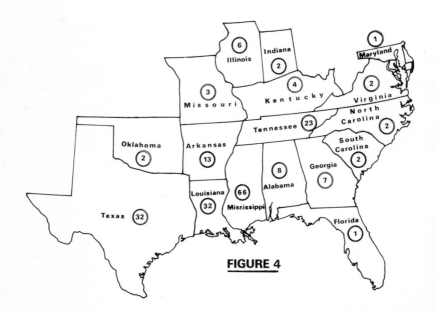

FIGURE 4

Mississippi, and that 'respondents from Mississippi, Arkansas, Tennessee and Alabama account for 75% of the sample' (Keil 1966: 155-6). Turning to the singers, Leadbitter and Slaven's *Blues Records: 1943-1966* lists the birth-places of 206 of the singers who recorded during these years. (These 206 form 30% of all blues singers who recorded from 1943-66.) Of these 206 singers, 71 made some or all of their records in Chicago, but of these 71, only 5 were born in Chicago. As Figure 4 shows, nearly all the recorded postwar singers were born in the Southern states. The evidence suggests that blacks born in Northern cities provide little support for blues.

Chicago: New York; Delta: Seaboard

Refining the gross distinction between North and South we find an extremely interesting picture. Within both North and South we find significantly variable support for blues. Chicago, and to a lesser extent Detroit, has, according to blues singers, promoters and radio station personnel, a much larger blues following than is found in New York and other northeastern cities. Blues singer and pianist Memphis Slim refers to this in his autobiographical *Boogying and Bluesing*. He sings of being born in Memphis, moving to East St Louis, then to Chicago, but when he went to New York,

> Finally I made Harlem and was I confused,
> My people there didn't dig no blues.

Ahmet Ertegun, head of New York-based Atlantic Records, discovered the dearth of blues singers in that city. He recalls from the early '50s, 'I was looking for a natural blues singer, and they're very hard to come by in New York, and I didn't have the money to travel all over the country looking for a talent' (*Melody Maker* 16 December 1972: 44).

Enoch Gregory (WWRL) explains the reasons for this differing support for blues in the North,

> Chicago's a funny place. I lived there for a year and a half when I worked at WBEE. The blues in later years have remained a musical entity more in the states of Mississippi, Alabama and some parts of Louisiana and Arkansas, rather than in North Carolina, Virginia, South Carolina, Georgia and Florida. The migration pattern has a good deal to do with it. The people in Mississippi and Alabama and those states go up to Chicago. The people in the coastal states come to Baltimore, Washington D.C., and primarily New York. So you find a deep appreciation for blues in Chicago, and in spite of attempted revivals by programme directors and show promoters here in New York, it does not exist in New York.

Three major routes of black migration from the South have developed. One, from the Delta states to Chicago and the Midwest, has already been examined. A second runs north along the Atlantic Seaboard to the northeast. From 1955 to 1960, 50% of non-white migrants to New York's metropolitan area came from North Carolina, South Carolina, Virginia, Georgia and Alabama, with North Carolina supplying 20% of New York's non-white immigrants (National Advisory Commission 1968: 240). A third route which will be referred to shortly runs westward to the West Coast.

Did blues remain more of a 'musical entity' in the Deep South rather than the Seaboard states, as Gregory suggests? The distribution according to birthplace of 206 postwar recorded bluesmen is shown in Figure 4. Almost one third of these singers and musicians was born in Mississippi and over half was born in the three main Delta states of Mississippi, Louisiana and Arkansas. Taking the six Eastern Seaboard states from Florida in the south to Maryland in the north, only 15 of the 206 singers were born in these states.

Relating these facts to the general migration pattern, we find that

STATE	number of singers	CHICAGO	DETROIT	MEMPHIS
MISSISSIPPI	36	29	3	7
TENNESSEE	15	10		N.A.
ARKANSAS	12	9	1	1
LOUISIANA	18	6	1	1
TEXAS	16	6	1	
ALABAMA	6	2	1	
GEORGIA	4	2		
KENTUCKY	2	1	1	
VIRGINIA	1			
NORTH CAROLINA	2			
MISSOURI	2	1		
OKLAHOMA	2			
TOTALS	116	66	8	9

North Central (Midwest) — Chicago and Detroit

North East — New York — 15

West Coast — Los Angeles and Oakland — 38

singers and their audiences travelled, in the main, by the same routes to the same destinations. Figure 5 tabulates those singers who recorded outside their home states for the black market, and gives the locations of the recordings. Since singers usually recorded for companies based in their home towns—most postwar record companies were small independents, often serving only a local market—the place of recording gives a fairly good

Of the 206 singers (30% of all singers listed) whose states of birth are given in Leadbitter & Slaven, 116 made records for a black audience outside their home states. Some recorded in more than one location, as is apparent from the table. Towns outside their home states in which less than five of the 116 singers recorded are not included in the table.

NEW YORK	HOUSTON	LOS ANGELES	OAKLAND	TOTALS
2	1	2	2	47
3		1		15
	1	2	1	15
4	6	7	1	28
	N.A.	12	2	22
1		2		6
1	1	1		5
1				3
1				1
2				2
		1	1	3
		2	1	3
15	9	30	8	150

FIGURE 5

Location of recordings by blues singers who recorded outside their states of birth for a black audience, 1943 — 1966

indication of where blues were popular and which towns the singers migrated to. From 1948-66 over three quarters of the singers born in Mississippi who recorded outside that state made some or all of their records in Chicago, and over half of all singers who recorded outside their home states made records in Chicago. Figure 5 also shows the importance of the West Coast as a blues centre. From 1955-60, 75% of non-white migrants to Los Angeles came from the states of Texas, Louisiana, Mississippi, Arkansas and Alabama (National Advisory Commission 1968: 240). Again the importance of blues at the point of origin of migrants is reflected at their destination.

We have discovered a relatively high incidence of blues in the Delta and Chicago, linked by migration, and a low incidence on the Eastern Seaboard and New York, also linked by migration. It has already been suggested that blues in Chicago has functioned as a transitional vehicle for rural migrants adapting to urban life. If blues functioned as an ongoing adaptational vehicle for black urban life in general, we should also expect it to enjoy similar popularity in New York. Both New York's Harlem and Chicago's South Side ghettoes produce similar problems for their residents. Since there is little support for blues in New York, this supports the thesis that blues is largely a survival from the mainly rural South. The explanation of why blues is more popular in Chicago than New York is simply because it is more popular in the Delta than in the Seaboard states.

To begin to understand the major function of blues, it is to this differing support for the music in the South that we must address ourselves. In looking at the question of why blues is more popular in some parts of the South than in others, we may approach more clearly the social and economic conditions to which blues was, and to some degree still is, a response.

From all indications Mississippi is the most important state for blues. It is generally recognised by blacks as the worst state in the Union for the severity of its application, and the pervasive nature, of the Jim Crow system—the legally backed and culturally sanctioned system of social, economic and political discrimination against and subordination of blacks. Mississippi led the South in instituting the Jim Crow system and put up the most prolonged and violent resistance to the civil rights legislation of the '50s and '60s. Even in 1970 Charles Evers of Fayette, Mississippi's first black mayor, could say with some justification about his commitment to civil rights, 'This is Mississippi and we are black. If I was a sharecropper, I would be dead in a ditch or run out of town a long time ago' (*Look* 34: 14 [1970] : 26).

Throughout the 20th century, Mississippi has had the largest number of black farmers, one fifth of the national total even in 1959 after extensive migration (Beale 1966: 172). It has also had the largest number of sharecroppers, working on the extensive white-owned and -organised cotton plantations. The sharecropping system provided the most refined

Cotton pickers on the plantation of the Delta and Pine Land Company, Bolivar County, Mississippi, October 1941.

and efficient method of black subordination. The plantation owner provides the tenant with land and credit. After the harvest, the owner deducts from the profits the cost of food, fuel, seed, fertiliser, and other sundry expenses such as medical bills, which the cropper has obtained on credit. The owner then splits the remaining profit 50:50 with his tenant. As often as not the tenant was informed that he was still in debt and was thus tied to the owner for at least a further year to work off his debt. The system was clearly open to abuse, and tenants were cheated, but data is not available to determine the extent of this abuse. Under the threat of the sanctions of Jim Crow, the cropper could not question the owner's accounting. Sharecropping resulted in a system of control and dependency that was practically feudal. Economic dependency reinforced by the Jim Crow system effectively subordinated thousands of black sharecroppers. A migrant describes the effect of this patron-client relationship, as he leaves a plantation in 1967 to go North.

Back in Mississippi I was 48 years old, but I was still like a child. I needed the white man for protection. If the coloured man had that, he could keep out of lots of trouble. He could get credit. He could do lots of things, lots of things. But he just had to have that protection. If you didn't have that protection, all kinds of things could happen, all kinds of things, just like could happen to a child without a daddy. (Bagdikian 1967: 64).

The Mississippi Delta is the poorest area in the United States. A report published in 1970 by the US Department of Agriculture reads:

The Mississippi Delta region has about the highest percentage of poor rural people among the areas of the United States . . . 79% of the Negro households and 84% of the Negro population were poor contrasted with 28 and 31% for whites . . . (Agricultural Economic Report 1970: viii).

In 1966 the median income for black households in the Delta was $1,373 (ibid: 29). This compares with the 1968 median for black households in the South of $4,278 and the national black average of $5,359 (Bureau of Labor Statistics 1970: 15).

In the field, the cotton is carried to the scales by mule (below: Washington County, Miss., 1941) and weighed (top right: Shelby, Miss., 1941). At the gin it is baled and weighed (centre right: Pointe Coupee parish, La., 1947) and loaded on to wagons (bottom right: Calvert, Tx., 1941).

Above: *handling cotton at the Tuskegee warehouse, Macon County, Ala.,
1940.* Right: *tobacco leaf is unloaded from the bulk curing racks, North
Carolina, 1973.*

Mississippi has the most virulent and efficient Jim Crow system, the
largest number of sharecroppers, and the highest incidence of black
poverty in the nation. It has also produced more blues singers than any
other state and black Mississippians, whether at home or in Chicago, form
the backbone of the blues audience. We suggest that blues is directly
related to the Jim Crow system and poverty. The nature of that
relationship, the function of blues as a response and adaptation to this
situation, will be developed in the next chapter.

Turning to the Eastern Seaboard states and in particular to North
Carolina, which has always had a large indigenous black population, we
find support for the thesis advanced above. During and since the time of
slavery, North Carolina has had a less repressive and vicious system of race
relations than the Delta states (Phifer 1968: 74-93). From 1882 to 1951,
84 blacks were lynched in North Carolina, compared with 534 for the

same period in Mississippi. The figure for Mississippi is the highest for the South, whereas only the border states of Virginia and Missouri have fewer black lynchings than North Carolina (Franklin and Starr 1967: 186-7). Further, the sharecropping system was less common in North Carolina and blacks were less dependent on white favour and support. Economically they were substantially better off than their counterparts in Mississippi. Throughout the Eastern Seaboard from northern Florida to North Carolina, tobacco farming expanded during the first half of the 20th century. Tobacco farming requires little land and was well suited to the many black-owned small farms which would have been uneconomic with other crops. From 1910 to 1945, non-white farm owners and tenants growing tobacco rose from 42,000 to 91,000. Black-operated farms growing tobacco are more likely to be operated by owners, to produce on a commercial scale, and yield higher profits, than those producing cotton. North Carolina is the most important tobacco state, it is now second only to Mississippi in its numbers of black farmers, and the value of its black-operated farms is higher than in any other state (Beale 1966: 169-70). These facts support the predicted relationship of blues to poverty and Jim Crow. Only 2 of the 206 blues singers in our sample who recorded

Left: *tobacco leaves are tied into hands, in preparation for market, at Lexington, Ky., a centre of Burley tobacco production.* Right: *after auction, the tobacco is packed and shipped to the processing factory. Here, packers at the Upper Marlboro, Md. market are packing the leaf into hogsheads for trucking to the factory.*

from 1943-66 were born in North Carolina. Blues finds relatively little support in New York City, which receives more black migrants from North Carolina than from any other state.

It is noteworthy that the blues of the Seaboard states differed not only in quantity but also in quality from those of the Delta. Paul Oliver states with reference to country blues that Seaboard and Border state singers place 'more importance on a sweet-flowing instrumental line than on any deep emotional involvement in the words' (Oliver 1971: 11). We may suggest that blues in the Seaboard states functioned more as simply entertainment than the Delta blues, which, as we shall illustrate in the following chapter, were more closely related to the pressures and pain produced by the circumstances of Delta blacks.

Beginning with the Blues

From Mississippi and North Carolina we have seen a directly proportional relationship between Jim Crow, poverty and blues. The greater the severity of Jim Crow, and the higher the incidence of poverty, the greater the popularity of blues. If blues is primarily a response to Jim Crow and poverty, we ought to find that blues began and developed with these factors. The evidence suggests that this is the case.

The date of the origin of blues is tentative, but the two foremost authorities on early blues place it around 1890 (Oliver 1960: 22; Charters 1967: 32). W.C. Handy first recalls hearing a blues sung in Cleveland, Mississippi, in 1895. Samuel Charters writes, 'It is the earliest moment at which someone remembers hearing the blues in the South and it could have been in the Delta that blues finally emerged as a musical style, distinct from the field hollers and the gang song of the rest of the rural South' (Charters 1967: 32). Accepting 1890 as the date for the origin of blues and the following ten or twenty years as the period in which the form was developed and dispersed, we find the predicted correlation with particularly severe poverty and Jim Crow.

The Jim Crow system did not appear immediately after the Civil War (1865). Reconstruction in the South led many blacks to hope for civil rights and equality and a general betterment of their situation. The first Civil Rights Act was passed in 1875, and decreed that blacks had the right to equal use of and accommodation in public transport and places of public entertainment. The Act was poorly enforced but it did offer hope. Blacks fared considerably better in politics. They were elected to every Southern legislature, 20 blacks served in the House of Representatives and two black Senators represented Mississippi (National Advisory Commission 1968: 213). C. Vann Woodward writes that in the 1870s

> Negroes still voted in large numbers, held numerous elective and appointive offices, and appealed to the courts with hope of redress of grievances ... It was a time of experiment, testing and un-certainty—quite different from the time of repression and rigid uniformity that was to come toward the end of the century. (Vann Woodward 1966: 33).

The 1880s and 1890s brought hardship and Jim Crow. There was a severe agricultural depression in the 1880s which continued into the 1890s and a more general economic depression in the 1890s (Vann Woodward 1966: 71, 81). Throughout the 1890s and 1900s the Jim Crow system was legislated and institutionalised until it pervaded every area of Southern life. Lynchings, the most overt and brutal form of black suppression, reached their highest incidence during the last two decades of the 19th century, averaging around one hundred annually and reaching a peak of 161 in 1892 (National Advisory Commission 1968: 216). Pioneered by Mississippi, the systematic disenfranchisement of blacks proceeded throughout the 1890s and 1900s. In 1896 there were 130, 334 registered black voters in Louisiana, by 1904 they numbered 1,342 (Vann Woodward 1966: 85). Blacks were excluded from skilled trades and white-collar jobs by employers and trade unions alike. The segregation laws of the 1900s ratified with the sanction and majesty of the law customary practices which had become increasingly common over the past decade. The system of 'repression and rigid uniformity' was complete, the advances of blacks were reversed, and their hopes for civil rights and equality dashed.

Against this background blues originated and developed. Relegated to the nadir of American society and maintained there with ruthless efficiency, black Americans were powerless to act against the system. They could do little but live under it and sing how they felt.

> Did you ever wake up with the blues and didn't have no place to go
> And you couldn't do nothin' but just walk from door to door?
>
> (Otis Harris, *Waking Blues*)

REGAL

47th & South Parkway

NEWLY REMODELED

Saturday & Sunday
AUG. 3-4

SHOWS SATURDAY 7:00 - 10:00 & 12:00 P. M.
SUNDAY SHOWS 7:00 & 10:00 P. M.

INTERNATIONAL BLUES FESTIVAL
For King of the Blues

B. B. KING

BOBBY BLAND

LITTLE MILTON
JUNIOR PARKER - ALBERT KING

★ **EXTRA ATTRACTION SATURDAY ONLY** ★

COUNT BASIE
AND MANY OTHER STARS

Advance Tickets on Sale at Box Office or The Burning Spear, 5523 South State

2/Going Down Slow

'Live' at the Regal and Father Blues

A hot summer's evening on Chicago's sprawling black South Side, crowds line up along the side of the Regal Theatre on the corner of 47th and South Parkway. There is an air of anticipation as people filter through the foyer, pay their three dollars and take their seats. Expectant chatter is accompanied by two enormous fans, the Regal's air conditioning, which slowly creak round above the balcony. Junior Parker's band opens the proceedings, and the audience settles down to enjoy an evening with the blues.

From live performances of blues it is clear that both words and music have a deep meaning. At the Regal, members of the audience express their appreciation of the music, shouting words of encouragement to singer and musician, and voicing their agreement with and relation to the message of the song. Applause and shouts of 'Yeah' follow the first line of each song, affirming the lyrics and recognising an old favourite. A few of the many responses recorded during a performance by Bobby Bland include 'sure 'nuff', 'what you say', 'say it again', 'that's it', 'take your time, son', 'sing your song, man', 'sing it, Bobby'. From a B.B. King performance: 'tell it', 'that's the truth', 'that's alright', 'take it down, baby', 'sing the blues' and 'that's your song, B.B., sing it'. These phrases are typical of audience response at a blues concert, and although their form is standardised, their expression is spontaneous. People shout as the mood of the music and the moment strikes them. Although the context invites these responses, they are individual responses; shouting, chanting or singing in unison are rarely found at a blues show.

Certain phrases within a song are particularly evocative and draw a shared response from large numbers of the audience. Lines such as 'Have you ever been mistreated' from Junior Parker's *Five Long Years*, 'I've been down so long' from Albert King's *Down Don't Bother Me*, 'I'm here to tell you the feeling is gone' from Bobby Bland's *The Feeling Is Gone* and 'I gave you seven children, woman, now you wanna give 'em back' from B.B. King's *How Blue Can You Get* produce widespread and enthusiastic responses. Singers sometimes use the techniques of gospel music to draw their audience into their songs, and explicitly request participation. During *Blind Man*, Little Milton shouts, 'Do you know how I feel? I wanna tell you I feel like the blind man. Do you feel like I'm feelin'?' and he is answered by a roar of affirmation. In *That's Alright*, Junior Parker asks the rhetorical question, 'You like the words out there?' and during the same song asks, 'I wanna hear if I got a witness out there?' Both questions bring a chorus of 'yeah's. Little Milton explains the mutual encouragement of singer and audience, 'When you feel good you show them that you feelin' good and in return they'll feel good. And it keeps workin' like it bounce offa one rock to the next.'

The meaning of blues is within the form of the music as much as the content of the lyrics. A particular guitar phrase from B.B. King brings shouts of 'play it B.', 'play the blues.' Junior Parker's harmonica introduction to *That's Alright* draws similar shouts of encouragement and approval. Wayne Bennett's guitar solo during Bobby Bland's *Stormy Monday* leads Bobby to request he 'say it again' and after a further twelve bars of cascading blue notes, Bobby typically turns to the audience and says 'Ain't that the truth', a comment which is echoed by many of the listeners. Musicians are conscious of speaking through their instruments. B.B. King states, 'When I'm not sayin' a word, I want my guitar to be able to sing, to say what I have in mind, and this is what I have tried to do.' Blues as music can crystallise and convey a mood and a message as effectively as a lyric. Disc-jockeys explain their own response. Lucky Cordell (WVON) says, 'When I say, "Ain't that the truth", it means you're playing the way I feel, you hit me right in the bag, the music you're playing is the truth, it's the blues.' Hal Atkins (WWRL) adds, 'You really feel what he's trying to say at that particular moment on the guitar.' Lee Garrett (WGPR) states simply, 'There are no words because it's a language in itself.'

Father Blues, 1641 West Roosevelt Road, on Chicago's black West Side, a club run by WVON DJs Pervis Spann and E. Rodney Jones: Albert King performs from 'nine until' on 6 July 1968. Excerpts from his performance illustrate the relationship between singer, song, music and audience.

'We're here until three' shouts Albert after the opening number, an up-tempo instrumental. 'We're with you' shout back several members of the audience. Albert peers from the brightly lit stage, 'There's some missing', he says. 'We're all here' shout back two or three people from one table. 'Yeah' shout several more reinforcing this response. Albert begins by setting the tone of the evening, the mutual support and empathy of performer and audience intermeshed in the ritual of a modern urban blues performance.

'I've been down so long' sings Albert, and scattered shouts of 'Yeah' and 'me too' greet the first line of *Down Don't Bother Me*. Several men raise their right arms, fists clenched, testifying to the blues. Albert talks over a guitar solo, 'We'll get together. Don't worry, don't worry about a thing. It's gonna be alright.' Singer and audience draw closer.

'Have to make the nights by myself', sings Albert. 'Sure 'nuff', yells back an onlooker. 'I have so much trouble, I can't hardly see my way.' 'That's the truth,' 'Tell it Albert', 'Yeah', exclaim various members of the

Right: *Albert King.*

audience. *'Born Under A Bad Sign'*, shouts a man requesting one of Albert's better known songs. His request is picked up and echoed by several others. 'Yes I was', replied Albert as he plays the introduction.

The audience is intent as Albert begins the fourth twelve-bar stanza of a guitar solo, building to a climax of intensity and volume. The drummer plays a roll, the organ holds a chord and the bass player thumbs the same note repeatedly as Albert lets out a whoop and bends a treble note on his guitar through one and a half tones. The band stops with a crash at the height of the crescendo, and Albert's blue note cuts through the haze of smoke and dim lights. The audience, completely involved in the moment, responds with an involuntary 'Oh!', an exclamation of complete release. A second later, a man standing, transfixed to the spot, shakes his head in disbelief; a woman throws her head from side to side over a glass of beer. The band quietly rejoins Albert, as he slides softly and sensuously up the frets of 'Lucy', his guitar, quietly and carefully playing the calm after the storm. The audience roars its appreciation of the contrast and its release from the intensity of the moment, with loud applause and shouts of 'play the blues'. Albert chuckles, 'That's called slippin' up on the blues.'

Few people leave before the end. By three o'clock everyone is filled with beer and blues. One man's comment as he leaves Father Blues summarises the mood. 'Man, I feel as mellow as I can be,' he smiles to a friend.

Audiences at blues performances clearly respond to both the form of the music and the content of the lyrics. They know the songs well and years of conditioning to the music have produced a readiness for response, which, in the charged and emotional atmosphere of a blues concert, is effectively triggered and released. Particular songs appear to crystallise the experiences of the listener and summarise his situation. Particular guitar phrases appear to reflect his mood and feelings. He involves himself within the performance and so becomes a part of it. Little Milton's request to the members of his audience to give themselves a round of applause recognises not only their financial support, but also their direct contribution to his performance: 'We want you to join with me and give the true stars of the show a big round of applause. When we say the true stars we are very sincere, 'cos we talkin' about you.'

What are the psychological effects of blues upon the listener? The music's main function appears to be cathartic, the release of tension through the expression of emotion. This release is effected by the relation of the individual's experience, much of it of a highly emotional nature, to the words of the song, mirrored and reflected in the musical accompaniment. Songs trigger memories of particular experiences or general moods which the individual draws from his past and releases into the present with exclamations of 'yeah'. Tensions from an individual's past and within him at the present are also released by another process. As the example of Albert King's guitar solo shows, tensions are created musically on the spot and then released within the same song. The singer manipulates the emotions of a willing audience and skilfully directs the process of catharsis. As audience response to blues reveals, both the experiences to which the lyrics relate, and the forms the responses to the music in general take, are shared. This facilitates the process of release and enhances and reinforces the cathartic effect, as the individual response becomes social, resulting in empathy and mutual support. The effect of this release is a feeling of well-being, of being cleansed, of feeling 'mellow'.

These observations and interpretations of the psychological functions of blues, based on data from live performances, may be validated and developed by comments from blues singers and disc-jockeys.

Tell the Truth and Live the Life

Black disc-jockeys maintain that a major feature of blues is its accurate and graphic depiction of individual experiences. As these experiences are sufficiently widespread, blues has a general application in voicing the overall situation. Ray Henderson (WCHB) says, 'I don't feel badly about the blues. It's like Ray Charles' record of *Tell The Truth* and that's what the blues is really doing. The blues is laying it down the line.' Jay Butler (WCHB) says, 'When B.B. King sings a blues song, he tells it just like it is.' Hal Atkins (WWRL) adds, 'Sometimes I say on the radio, "Blues ain't nothing but the truth", and that's actually what it is. It's a true experience in life.'

The belief in the 'truth' of blues is reinforced by the belief that the singer has experienced what he is singing about. Fred Goree (WCHB) summarises this view.

> Blues means like you have to have been through it, you have to have experienced it . . . If an artist can project the blues, more than ninety per cent of the time, he's experienced everything he's singing about, and to really get the true picture, and the true feeling, an artist really has to have been through this kind of thing.

Blues singers confirm these points. They have lived the life from which they distil the truth. Junior Parker states, 'Most of the things we sing about actually have happened to us, or to a neighbour, so this is what we go by.' Personal experience and direct observation form the basis of B.B. King's songs: 'I've seen many people hurt, homes broken, people killed, people talked about, so today I sing about it.' John Lee Hooker states, 'Blues is a story, it tells a story of life, what people are going through and what their problems are. I sing about my own experiences, what other people experience, and what they are going through.' Albert King echoes the above comments but adds wryly, 'But I wouldn't be here today if it all happened to me.' Bobby Bland puts as much emphasis on his cultural background and musical socialisation as his personal experiences: 'More or less I'm telling my own story, because if you don't know about it, you

Bobby Bland—an early publicity photograph.

can't sing about it. But I didn't have a real hard time actually. It was just the environment and growing up with the music.' These statements by urban blues singers apply equally to rural blues, as the remarks of country blues singers recorded by Samuel Charters illustrate; Furry Lewis, '. . . all the blues you can say is true'; J.D. Short, '. . . and there's so many true words in blues, of things that have happened to so many people, and that's why it makes the feeling in the blues'; Henry Townsend, 'You can only express what happened to you' (Charters 1963: 12).

In relation to an audience, a successful blues song presupposes shared experiences. Lyrics generally refer to situations that have effected most people. Singers emphasise the importance of reflecting shared experience and explain how individuals relate to a situation expressed in song. B.B. King states,

> When I sing a blues the whole song may not be about the person, but there are certain things in it that they will recognise that have happened to them, or some of their friends, and when this happens, they feel it.

Little Milton explains,

> Somebody hear 'em [blues] and they start screamin'. It reminds
> them of something that has happened to them, or is still happenin'
> to 'em, and maybe they are anticipating that it will happen to 'em. I
> think this is why it moves people, because it's for real.

Bobby Bland describes a typical member of one of his club audiences: 'He
sits back and relaxes, and if he got himself a little bottle, he can sip and
reminisce over some of his past.'

The blues singer publicly expresses the problems and feelings of the
individual. He thus represents his audience, he sings in the first person, and
performing on stage is, in a sense, his audience writ large. This role of the
blues singer has been particularly important, for, until recently, representation of the black lower classes in America has been virtually
non-existent. Little Milton relates what members of his audiences over the
years have told him:

> Some fans say we were like spelling out a thing that they had wanted
> to say, but then on the other hand it's kind've impossible to express
> it to the whole world what your situation really is, so I've tried to do
> my best to try . . . Some people don't have nobody and it's a thing
> where you can feel you being represented.

Junior Parker alludes to the importance of blues as one of the few means
available to black Americans for telling the world how they felt. 'A lot of
the time, that was the only way we could express ourselves, through song
y'know.'

You Get It Off Your Chest

As we have seen from the analysis of live performances, a major function
of blues appears to be emotional catharsis, a releasing and purging process
which produces a feeling of relief and well-being. Ed Cook (WVON) likens
blues to alcohol in its effect: 'Hearing the blues is just like having a drink,
more than one.' Little Milton states, 'As the old folks used to tell me, you
get it off your chest, you feel better.' Singers quoted by Paul Oliver
explain this function of blues: Robert Curtis Smith, 'I love the blues
because the blues is the only thing that gives me relief when I gets to the
place where it seems like everything go wrong'; Boogie Woogie Red, 'Blues
is something that relax your nerves'; Henry Townsend, 'It give you
relief—it kinda helps somehow'; Lil Son Jackson, 'I can get vexed up or
somethin' or I have a sad feelin'; seems like to me that if I can sing, I feel
better' (Oliver 1965: 23, 24, 34).

A further psychological function of blues is closure, a satisfying
characterisation and categorisation of experience. Encapsulated within the
time-tested phrases of a blues song, experience is organised and, as Little
Milton states, 'spelt out', and the audience accepts this definition of its

situation with shouts of 'that's it', 'that's the truth,' When a malady is labelled, a difficult experience classified, anxiety and tension are reduced because order is created out of disorder. Without a name, that is a symbol, a thing doesn't really exist. A name confirms its existence, makes it knowable and comprehensible, and establishes it within a society's culture, which means everybody knows about it. Indefinable feeling states are translated into homespun concepts such as 'the blues'. Songs such as B.B. King's *Everyday I Have The Blues* name the malady, define the mood, and state that the feeling is a common, everyday experience. By providing categories which encapsulate and symbolise experience, blues in particular and culture in general organise and give meaning to that experience. Disparate experiences may be related and their essential nature represented by the concept of 'the blues'. This is a public concept which everybody can relate to and it provides a means of communicating and sharing feelings. Within a phrase, blues songs summarise experience and what people feel about that experience. In this sense we may speak about blues effecting closure.

Bobby Bland states, 'People have particular songs that make them reminisce about when they were doing such and such and sometimes it puts them back together. Well, I think the blues does this.' Whether the song itself recalls the memory because it was first heard in the context or at the time of the event, or a particular phrase within the song recalls the event, the past is brought into the present. Every individual throughout his life organises and reorganises his past experience. Blues sometimes acts as a catalyst for this process. By evoking past experience, often by means of a particular phrase such as 'I've been down so long that down don't bother me,' blues also organises and summarises experience in terms of that phrase. The past is integrated into the present and experience is given continuity by the summary. We may refer to this process which includes closure, as personal re-integration—blues triggers the memory, recalls experiences, summarises them, effects closure, and integrates the past with the present. Personal re-integration puts people 'back together'.

A blues concert illustrates the social psychology of the individual psychological processes of catharsis, closure and personal re-integration. It is often within this emotionally charged social context that these processes operate most effectively. The listener experiences the sympathy and understanding of others, for they are responding to his problem. As Little Milton says, 'They can say, "Well, here's a cat that understands".' Solidarity and mutual support are fostered as the singer and audience encourage and reinforce one another by voicing their relation to the particular problem. The context invites members of the audience to express how they feel, knowing that others feel the same way. Individual problems and feelings are seen to be social. Again quoting Little Milton, 'They can say "Like here's a cat that feel the same way I do".' Shared responses of 'Yeah' and 'That's the truth' tends to define problems not only as shared but as commonplace and normal events. The perception of problems as shared and normative makes them easier to bear and reduces anxiety about them. As Butterball (WVON) puts it, 'A person say, "Well, I'm just paying my dues like everybody else. So I've had a rough time, but so has this guy and that guy." So now it becomes commonplace and the impact or the pain of it is less intense.' Finally, the shared affirmation of a definition of a problem encourages the individual to accept that definition. The production of knowledge is a social process and the definition of the situation contained in B.B. King's *Everyday I Have The Blues* has been part of black American culture for over half a century.

It is useful to view a blues concert as ritual. As the participants in a ritual event, members of a blues audience come together in shared communion. The ceremony is standardised, the audience knows the songs and has seen the singers many times before. Responses to the performance are patterned. Truths, not necessarily eternal, but certainly longstanding— many phrases sung today are echoed in blues recorded in the '20s—are articulated, and the audience testifies to their validity. The atmosphere, though not necessarily reverential, is highly charged. Just as participants in a religious ritual often depart cleansed and made whole, so members of a blues audience depart 'mellow' and 'put back together'. Religious rituals are largely conservative and, backed by myths and eternal verities, they define what life, and man's role within it, is and shall be. Blues performs a similar function, a point that will be developed later in this chapter.

Blues and the Alley

Traditionally blues has been the music of lower-class black Americans, the mass of the black population. Although still small in relation to white society, the size and proportion of the black middle and upper classes has grown steadily. Many blacks associate music with class and status groupings, as noted in the previous chapter. Some informants suggest that the decline in popularity of blues is due to the growth of the black middle class and what they see as the increasing desire of many low-income blacks for middle-class respectability. Some suggest that not only do many blacks wish to dissociate themselves from the lower classes, but they also want to associate themselves with white America. They thus reject blues as ethnic music. Ed Cook (WVON) puts this view: 'Personally I blame it on the so-called middle-class Negro, who wanted to identify with white society so much that he thought that there was something to be ashamed of about blues.' Before assessing these views it is necessary to examine some of the associations blacks have with blues.

Before playing the harmonica introduction to *That's Alright*, Junior Parker shouts to the audience, 'Alright, we're gonna keep it in the alley' and the audience yells back, 'Yeah, we're with you.' Many blacks associate blues with the alley, with drunkenness, violence, gambling, profanity, sexual promiscuity, ignorance and lack of education, and with the lowest stratum of black society. To some extent these associations hold whether the listener accepts or rejects the music. A man stands in a record shop on Plymouth Avenue, the main street running through the Minneapolis North Side ghetto, listening to a slow blues by Bobby Bland. Turning to his companion, he says, 'Don't that remind you of sitting on a bar room stool. Yeah, I'm gonna buy that record.' Jack Harris, a disc-jockey on KUXL, Minneapolis, shouts during Otis Rush's *Gambler's Blues,* 'Pass the corn whisky, let me have a swig.' Playing *The Woman I Love* by B.B. King, E. Rodney Jones of WVON says, 'You know the best moonshine comes from Arkansas.' After *I'm Shorty*, a song in which Tommy Tucker boasts about his sexual conquests, Ed Cook (WVON) says, 'Yeah, I'm the fox, the sly fox that nobody pays attention to but I'm the one who does all the damage.' These responses are sometimes to the lyrics but more generally reflect the associations of the music.

The class and status associations with blues are aptly illustrated by the local assessment of bars in the Minneapolis North Side ghetto. The Blue Note Lounge, the Cozy Bar and Lounge and the Regal Tavern are ranked by North Side residents in terms of their respectability. They are also distinguished by the type of music they feature. The Blue Note, judged the most respectable, presents jazz, usually the Frank Edwards Trio or other local bands, playing in the style of Brother Jack McDuff and Jimmy McGriff. The Cozy features soul music and occasionally brings in nationally known blues singers such as Muddy Waters and Junior Parker. The Cozy is ranked between the Blue Note and the Regal. The Regal Tavern is judged by one and all to be the least respectable of the three bars. It is the only bar that regularly features blues. In 1966 and 1967 a blues band led by Mojo Buford played four nights a week. Known locally as the Bucket of Blood, the Regal was seen as a place where brawls and 'shootin's and cuttin's' were common, and as a hangout for prostitutes. There is evidence to support this characterisation. The Regal was closed by the police from time to time after shootings, and reopened after a cooling-off period. Observations include a man cleaning a .38 pistol in the gentlemen's toilet and an argument between a group of men which ended with one of them running out of the Regal shouting, 'I'm gonna get my motherfuckin' Winchester.' Local prostitutes are a common sight and sound at the Regal, and some go to the Blue Note on their nights off. As a background to the arguments, fights, and business transactions of the girls, the blues band plays on. Similar evidence comes from Chicago and Detroit. The area of Chicago's South Side in which Theresa's (48th and Indiana) and Turner's (39th and Indiana), both famous Chicago blues bars, are situated is considered by many as one of the worst areas for violence and crime. 'I wouldn't never go there' is a comment heard from more than one South Side resident. Prince Hall on Gratiot and McDougall, one of the main venues for blues in Detroit, is situated in the poorest area of the East

*Mojo graduates from the Regal to the Cozy. Mojo Buford (*right*) and Sonny Boy Rogers at the Cozy Bar, Minneapolis, March 1970.*

Side ghetto. As Joe Scott's band is playing, a member of the audience says, 'This is the lowest place where soul is at. This is the black bottom neighbourhood. I know these people, they're my people. They're good people unless they done wrong, then they get mad, real mad.' His statement is prophetic. Bobby Bland, advertised to appear, fails to show and the audience wrecks Prince Hall, smashing tables and chairs, and attempts to set fire to the band's bus parked outside. The poverty of many members of the audience is clear from their remarks, 'Man, I spent my last three dollars gettin' this suit outta the cleaners for this show. I'm gonna sit here till I gets my money back if it takes all night.'

Blues singers are seen to personify the 'down in the alley' associations of the music. 'You mean that bum who used to sit drinking on the street corner,' was one man's response to the mention of Little Walter in Theresa's. Muddy Waters' appearance at the Cozy Bar, Minneapolis, occasioned a discussion of the forty scars he was supposed to have on his chest from various knife fights. When Bobby Bland failed to appear at Prince Hall, Detroit, various rumours swept the audience. He was in jail for not paying maintenance, he was running from a paternity suit, he was in bed with a woman, he had been seen in his gold lamé suit, too drunk to sing, peeping through the stage curtains, supported by his aides. The truth of these assertions does not concern us here. They do however illustrate the oft-cited stereotypes which surround the blues singer. Singers are aware of the image which accompanies their profession. Talking about blues, B.B. King says, 'It was almost like a bad taste in your mouth, almost like using profanity . . . if you said blues it was almost like a guy was illiterate completely, he didn't know anything, and this was the lowest form of music . . .' (*Melody Maker* 1 May 1971: 35). Detroit blues singer Little Sonny attacks the stereotype: 'The idea that a man has to use foul language, dress raggedy and bummy, and get into cuttin' and shootin' scrapes in order to sing the blues is just a sham. I've had my share of hard times, but that doesn't give me an excuse to drink and swear and cut up.' (Stax Public Relations (1) n.d.: 1).

The lyrics of blues provide ample illustration of and support for the 'down in the alley' associations. Lines such as 'I can't read, I didn't learn how to write' and 'You know wine and women is all I crave' from Albert King's *Born Under A Bad Sign* crop up with minor variations in many blues songs. The boastful lover and the promiscuous 'back door man' are standard blues themes. In *I'm Shorty* Tommy Tucker announces his prowess as a lover and boasts of his success with other men's wives. On the other side of the coin Lightnin' Hopkins sings in *Back Door Friend*

> What you gonna do with a married woman,
> When she got a back door friend,
> When she's just prayin' for you to move out,
> So her back door friend can move in.

Louisiana Johnny's response to mistreatment from his woman fits the stereotype. In *Razor Cuttin' Man* he threatens,

> I'm goin' to buy me a razor,
> Baby just for myself,
> I'm gonna cut you until
> You won't even know yourself.

Blues and the bottle are often in association. In *Corn Likker Blues* Leroy Carr makes no bones about his fondness for alcohol.

> I love my good corn likker,
> And I really mean I do.
> Now I don't care who knows it,
> And I really mean that too.

B.B. King sings a typical blues couplet describing *The Woman I Love.*

> I say my baby likes the moonshine,
> Like most people love to eat.

Residing on the lowest rung of the social ladder is a typical backdrop in blues. In *Born Under A Bad Sign* Albert King sings,

> Born under a bad sign,
> Been down since I began to crawl.

In *I'm Just A Bum* Big Bill Broonzy states simply,

> I am just a bum, woman,
> I have to sit up all night long,
> Lord I'm just a poor boy,
> Lord and I ain't got no home.

Blues singers suggest that blacks aspiring to middle-class status reject blues because of the music's 'down in the alley' associations. They imply that these attitudes are the product of superficial social conventions and that those who say they don't like blues are not being true to themselves. Junior Parker states,

> I would go as far as to say I think all Negroes like the blues. You will have some that say they don't dig blues, but you go to their home and you find some blues records. They may try to get in a different bag and say they don't. But we have played some very nice clubs and we have had some Negro people sitting there saying, 'We don't like the blues', and later on that night they get high and then it comes out of them.

B.B. King echoes this view: 'I've had black people to tell me, "I've never listened to the blues; I've never liked them." I think that's an exaggeration. I believe that deep down in, every black person has got blues, and a lot of whites' (*Soul Sounds* 31 October 1968: 5).

It is important to note that the 'down in the alley' connotations have always been with blues. Traditionally it has been considered 'devil music' and 'sinful music' and there has been a sharp division between blues and gospel music as representing diametrically opposed ways of life. Since the negative associations have always been with blues, we cannot point to them in themselves as sufficient reasons for its decline.

The black middle and upper classes have traditionally taken great pains to dissociate themselves from the black lower classes. In the past 15 or so years, the increase in the size of the middle class, though significant, has not changed the fact that the vast majority of blacks still make up the lower classes. The relatively small numerical increase of the middle class hardly accounts for the large decrease in the popularity of blues. In fact the available evidence suggests that the only new black support for blues comes from this class. Taj Mahal, one of the very few young black blues singers who has risen to prominence in the past few years, comes from a middle-class family and has the unlikely background (for a blues singer) of an undergraduate career at a New York university training as a veterinary surgeon. His act consists of revamping old country blues and his audience mainly of white undergraduates on the college circuit. Since blues has become popular with the white middle class, members of the black middle class are observed in increasing numbers at concerts given by Muddy Waters and B.B. King at such chic and fashionable venues as the Tyrone Guthrie Theatre, Minneapolis (1969).

John Lee Hooker.

Turning from class to ethnicity we consider the argument that blues is rejected because it is black ethnic music. Jay Butler (WCHB) puts this view: 'Back in 1954, the black community didn't want to be associated with blues ... they wanted to be accepted by whites.' There is some evidence to suggest that in the middle and late '50s and early '60s, following the 1954 Supreme Court decision on school desegregation, many blacks identified with white society and consciously rejected the stereo-types associated with blackness, many of which are contained in the 'down in the alley' connotations of blues. Coupled with the expectation of acceptance into white society was a rejection of aspects of black culture which were specifically black, blues being a prime example. As John Lee Hooker says, 'Blues is our music, it's our trademark.' Insufficient evidence exists to evaluate this argument properly. However, it can be shown to be invalid from the middle '60s onwards. The emergence of black pride and a positive evaluation of black ethnicity stems from the mid-'60s. Were blues formerly rejected because of its ethnic associations, one would expect a resurgence of its popularity in the '60s. In fact just the opposite happened. The decline of blues releases begun in the mid-'50s has continued unabated. Reasons other than ethnicity appear to account for the decline in popularity of blues.

The final argument in this section states that many lower-class blacks have middle-class aspirations and so reject blues because of its 'down in the alley' connotations. These connotations, the argument goes, run counter to their image of middle-class respectability. Conversations with many lower-class blacks resulted in the impression that their concern is not so much with respectability and class status, but rather with self-improvement. They see the future in terms of better jobs, housing and education and this perspective is not directly associated with images of respectability. However, self-improvement does run counter to the 'down in the alley' associations of blues, and is the strongest argument for the rejection of blues specifically on those grounds. The way of life portrayed in many blues is something black Americans want to leave behind, not because it is unrespectable but rather because it is undesirable. Evidence to support this argument is given in Chapter 4. We conclude that the 'down in the alley' associations of blues are a factor in its decreasing popularity. Many lower-class blacks reject this way of life, not so much because they wish to associate with the middle class and gain social status, but rather because of a concern for self-improvement and an increasing refusal to live the life portrayed in many blues songs. This refusal is due to the belief that a better way of life is within the realm of possibility. The factors that have led to this belief are outlined in the final chapter.

Young Blacks and Blues

Ed Cook, a middle-aged disc-jockey at WVON, Chicago, and long-time supporter of blues, sits and talks despondently about the future of the music he loves.

> It's a shame. The teenager of the past ten years hasn't been exposed to blues. He doesn't know anything. It's like the Negroes not knowing their own history. And it's the adults' fault and the disc

jockeys' fault around the country. The younger breed of DJ knows nothing about the blues and it's a disgrace, it really is.

The attitude of most younger blacks to blues ranges from disinterest or amused tolerance to distaste. B.B. King tops the bill at the Regal Theatre and the younger members of the audience are walking out throughout his act. They had stayed to watch Little Milton who included soul songs in his performance, but B.B. King playing nothing but the blues does not appeal to them. A young man in his early 20s hears a blues record at a party; 'Hey', he smiles, 'They're playin' that old back porch jive my mama used to play down in Alabama.' A young black modern jazz quartet preceded John Lee Hooker's act at the Rapa House, Detroit. As John performs his four numbers, singing intensely and stomping his foot, the young musicians shout mock encouragement and slap their thighs in amusement as they crack jokes about the old blues singer. Talking after the show John Lee Hooker expresses annoyance about the 'come on's, gimme's and put on's' of many young blacks when presented with blues.

Black teenagers have little or no interest in blues. As B.B. King says, 'They don't even know about it, and when they do hear about it they think, "Well that's old mom and dad's music",' Their opinions about the music are summed up in phrases like 'That music don't mean nothing to me,' 'Don't know nothing about it,' and 'Those blues singers are always cryin',' 'They're always moanin'.' James Brown voices the opinion of many that blues has little or no musical value. 'Any kid can play the blues. I been playing music for a long time so I know what I'm talking about' (*Inbeat* June 1967: 17). B.B. King gives his view of the results of this attitude: 'I guess a lot of the people, especially young people, thought it was a low form of music, something that didn't require any skill or anything of that sort, so they just bypassed it' (*Melody Maker* 1 May 1971: 35).

Some singers and disc-jockeys suggest that blues is an acquired taste that develops with maturity and that the young will learn to appreciate the music. Junior Parker states, 'After they have to go to work on Monday morning and work five or six days and when they come home and have nothing left from the cheque, then they'll know what blues means.' Jay Butler (WCHB) supports this view that adult experience will lead to identification with blues:

> If you take B.B. King singing lines like, 'Don't want nobody around my house when my baby's not at home,' it doesn't have the meaning to the young ones because they haven't lived that part of it yet. Maybe when they get to thirty-five or forty years old and they've been married and had problems, then it will.

Joe Cobb gives a personal view of the transition to blues maturity: 'Once the teenagers get to a certain age they will learn to appreciate the blues. I was this way once. I only cared for the dance type soul music, but as I got older I began to care more too for blues.' Talking about the dearth of young blues singers, John Lee Hooker suggests, 'As they get older and begin to experience and see some part of the rough life, then they begin to develop into a deep blues singer. But right now they got a sharp edge on 'em. They wanna really swing all the time.'

Past precedents may uphold these views. Certainly the arguments seem reasonable. But the predictions are not materialising. Granted, the median age of the black population is getting lower, but the numbers of all ages are increasing. Blacks are reaching the age of 'blues maturity' every year, but blues continues to decline in popularity.

Blues is a feeling

'Blues is a story', says John Lee Hooker, 'and blues is a feelin', blues is a feelin'.' As a definition of blues music, the phrase 'blues is a feeling' is used by singers and blues fans alike. Blues does more than tell a story, it articulates a mood, a state of mind. Many blues lyrics recur with minor variations in hundreds of songs recorded over half a century. Their strength lies not in novelty but in their effectiveness in expressing a mood. Their standardised themes and phrases are as much a vehicle for expressing a state of mind as depicting a series of events. Their function is evocative as well as narrative. It is important to characterise this mood, the state of mind called 'the blues'. The following extracts from blues are presented followed by a composite picture of the mood they portray.

Hard Luck Blues by Roy Brown:

> I've got so much, so much trouble,
> Sometimes I sit and cry
> I'm gonna find my mother's grave,
> Fall on the tombstone and die.

Black Night by Charles Brown:

> Nobody cares about me,
> Ain't even got a friend,
> My baby's gone and left me,
> When will my troubles end,
> Black night is fallin',
> Oh how I hate to be alone,
> I keep cryin' for my baby,
> But now another day is gone.

Why Do Everything Happen To Me by B.B. King:

> I wonder why,
> Why do everything happen to me
> Well I'm blue and I'm lonesome,
> My heart is filled with misery.

Blues Pain by Lowell Fulsom:

> You know my mother's gone,
> Yes and my father too,
> My sister and my brother,
> I have no one left but you,
> Why mistreat me baby,
> By doin' the things you do,
> I'm just standin' all alone,
> The blues pain aches to the bone.

From these few short extracts it is possible to isolate a range of related moods and states of mind: sadness, misery, despair, loneliness and rejection, helplessness, hopelessness and resignation. Though the examples quoted above are particularly despondent, the feelings isolated form the central theme of blues, and are those noted by blacks when talking about blues. The mood presented has hung over black America for the best part of half a century. The standard and traditional formula of many blues lyrics bears witness to their power to reflect and express it. Again, it is important to recognise that this mood is as much a part of the music as the lyrics, they are inseparable in representing and articulating it. There is a similar standardisation in the structure of the music. The basic twelve-bar blues framework has carried the message of the blues since its inception. The relation of mood to music, the power of blues to capture and express exactly what the individual feels within a short phrase is vividly illustrated by Detroit disc-jockey Lee Garrett's earliest childhood memory. 'The first thing I remember was waking up one morning about four o'clock and hearing my brother sing a blues, *I Feel So Unnecessary*. It touched me and I wanted to imitate it, to learn it.'

Though most blues have overtones of sadness, there are some happy blues. These songs tend to be up-tempo dance numbers in which, relative to slow blues, the rhythm is more important than the words. Unlike up-tempo gospel songs, the lyrics are inclined to hedonism rather than hope. J.B. Lenoir's *I Feel So Good* is an example of an up-tempo happy blues.

> I feel so good,
> I don't know what to do,
> Babe I feel so good,
> I feel like I just wanna play wid you.

The few blues that express joy and happiness do so in spite of the general mood and situation rather than because of it. Little Milton explains this point:

> There are some happy blues. It's like in church. You be listening to a sermon that the preacher's preaching, and he build your hopes up man, so high, so high that you get happy although you had so many burdens and troubles when you got there. But this cat can talk so

much talk to you and get your hopes built up so you can still have the blues, but they can be happy ones.

In reflecting the general mood blues is also directive. As well as expressing how people feel, it also tells them how they ought to feel and how they should expect to feel. Generations of black Americans were raised with blues, their outlook moulded within its frame of reference before they experienced the events it described. Despite the adult themes many blues singers started as teenagers or even earlier. Junior Wells was playing his harmonica and singing blues on the streets of West Memphis, Arkansas, at the age of nine. At 13 Muddy Waters was singing and playing harmonica for 50 cents a night at Saturday night fish fries in Clarksdale, Mississippi. Robert Johnson was an established blues singer while still a teenager. Junior Parker played his first professional engagement with Sonny Boy Williamson (Rice Miller)'s band at the age of 16. B.B. King, who didn't start singing blues until he was demobbed from the Navy, was the exception rather than the rule. Many black Americans were literally born with the blues and lived and died within the decades when blues was popular. In expressing a mood of sadness, blues also promotes that mood and so helps to maintain it.

Blues and Jim Crow

There is scarcely a reference in blues to the Jim Crow system, despite the fact that it impinged daily on the lives of many black Americans. Paul Oliver writes, 'In the blues and its related forms there are few examples which even hint at racial intolerance, of white oppression, of segregation or violence as a result of prejudice' (Oliver 1968: 257). One of a handful of examples from country blues which refers to race relations is Tommy McClennan's *Bottle It Up and Go*, recorded in 1939:

> Now the nigger and the white man,
> Playin' seven up,
> Nigger beat the white man,
> Scared to pick it up,
> He had to bottle up and go.

In this and similar scattered examples there is no element of social protest. The relationship between black and white is merely described and summarised. Such examples may well be survivals from an earlier form of music. A verse very similar to the one quoted above was published in 1876, pre-dating blues by some ten or fifteen years (Oliver 1969: 21). Urban blues has nothing at all to say about race relations.

Despite this dearth of reference to race relations, there is evidence to suggest that blues is a direct response to the Jim Crow system. B.B. King explains what blues means to him,

Where I lived, a little place between Itta Bena and Indianola in Mississippi, the people are practically the same way today, they live practically that same way, and that is under the fear of the boss in a manner of speaking. Because so many Negroes down there have been killed many, many different types of ways if you said the wrong thing at the wrong time. Very few were able to get away with speaking up with what they thought was right or what was wrong. So when they use the word frustration, I don't think that really tells the whole story because a guy get to feeling a lot of times he's afraid, he's actually afraid. They use the word brainwash, because if you live under that system for so long, then it don't bother you openly, but mentally, way back in your mind it bugs you . . . Later on you sometime will think about all of this and you wonder why, so that's where your blues comes in, you really bluesy then, y'see, because you are hurt deep down, believe me, I've lived through it, I know. I'm still trying to say what the blues is to me. So I sing about it. The next thing, which is relatively minor compared to living like I have, is your woman. Y'see your woman is the next thing that can make a man pretty blue too y'know.

B.B. King suggests that the primary importance of blues is as a response to the Jim Crow system. Yet in his songs he has nothing to say about the system as such. Nearly all his songs are about men and women, the problems of their relationships and the pain and misery this produces. How then is blues related to the system? There are two possible answers to this question. First, many blues may act as metaphors for the system. The vehicle of a man-woman relationship may represent the relationship of black and white, the allegories of hardship may stand for the operation of the Jim Crow system. Thus the song *Five Long Years* with the words

> Have you ever been mistreated,
> Then you know what I'm talking about,
> I worked five long years for one woman,
> Then she had the nerve to put me out.

Five Long Years by Eddie Boyd.
© 1952 Frederick Music Company. Used by permission.

may represent the ill-treatment and injustice of the Jim Crow system Discussing this possibility, Junior Parker, who recorded *Five Long Years* and featured it regularly in his stage act, says: 'No, I disagree on that, I don't think it's based like that. This is just based on a couple who can be together for so many years and they scuffle together. Then they started getting along bad and he gets put out.'

Evidence does however exist for the interpretation of a song on more than one level, and in particular the translation of a man-woman relationship into terms of the wider framework of race relations. Little Milton's *We're Gonna Make It* is a case in point.

The late Junior Parker: early publicity photograph for Duke Records (left) and last such, for Groove Merchant Records.

> We may not have a cent to pay the rent,
> But we gonna make it, I know we will,
> We may have to eat beans every day,
> But we gonna make it, I know we will,
> And if a job is hard to find,
> And we have to stand in the welfare line,
> I got your love and you got mine,
> So we gonna make it, I know we will.

The record was released in 1965 at the height of the civil rights movement. Little Milton recalls the unexpected results.

> We got involved in this racial issue at the time when *We're Gonna Make It* came out, and this was like a hopeful tune. Now when we did this we had no thoughts, none at all, concerning the great Reverend Martin Luther King's movement which at that time was really beginning to pick up oodles of momentum. We were just trying to get a hit record man, y'know. But it was a tune that everybody could see was reaching for hope, for a brighter tomorrow, and it spelt out this. But we were talking about one man talkin' to his woman and if they kept pullin' and pushin' that they would make it.

Similarly *I'm Gonna Push On* by Charles Brown has been related, at least by a disc-jockey who played it in 1968, to the civil rights issue.

> I'm gonna push on,
> A little longer,
> Satisfy my soul,
> Until I reach my goal.

Ed Cook (WVON) comments after the record, 'Yeah, you'd better believe it,' and explains his remark when interviewed, 'Well, it's in reference to me and the people who listen to me . . . and what we're striving for, the civil rights fight in other words.'

Several points about those songs deserve mention before developing the main argument. Firstly, neither are typical of blues in terms of words or music. *We're Gonna Make It* is closer to gospel music than to blues, featuring a call and response chorus in the closing bars. The use of the first person plural rather than singular is a feature of soul music, not of blues. Charles Brown's *I'm Gonna Push On* is a blues ballad rather than a blues and its lyrics find few precedents in more traditional blues. Secondly, listeners are relating these songs to events which were unknown in the heyday of blues. It is their coincidence in time with the civil rights movement that probably results in this particular interpretation. Were they played in the '20s and '30s when blacks had little or no hope of effectively opposing the Jim Crow system, they would probably have not been interpreted in terms of race relations.

Accepting the above reservations, these examples do admit the possibility of more than one level of meaning in blues. They show how a formal message may be abstracted from the content of the story and related to other situations. In this way it is possible to see how blues may have referred to Jim Crow when that system was relatively impregnable. However, interviews and conversations with blues singers and blues fans, many of whom grew up under Jim Crow in the South, failed to produce further examples of a formal message in blues being abstracted and explicitly related to race relations. If this process occurred before civil rights agitation caught the imagination of black Americans, it was probably on a subconscious level. Muddy Waters' retrospective statement about his early days in Mississippi is probably the best assessment of the relationship between blues, the thought processes of the singer and audience, and the Jim Crow system.

> I can't remember much of what I was singin' now 'ceptin' I do remember I was always singin', 'I cain't be satisfied, I be all troubled in mind.' Seems to me like I was always singin' that, because I was always singin' jest the way I felt, and maybe I didn't exactly know it, but I jest didn't like the way things were down there—in Mississippi. (Oliver 1965; 30).

Without denying the possibility that individuals may have related

Little Milton.

particular blues to the system, it seems reasonable to conclude that traditionally, blues in general were not thinly disguised metaphors for the Jim Crow system.

A second argument provides a more satisfactory answer to the question of the realtionship of blues and Jim Crow. This argument allows us to take the lyrics of blues more at their face value. It accepts B.B. King's statement that he sings about the system in the sense that he articulates the moods and feelings produced by it. It accepts the universal statement of blues singers that they sing the way they feel, and the assertion of performer and audience alike that blues is a feeling. Referring back to the section which isolated the feeling states in blues, we can see clearly that they are the very feelings that result from the operation of the Jim Crow system. As B.B. King says, the system causes the 'hurt deep down', it 'don't bother you openly but way back in your mind it bugs you'. This feeling and state of mind is reflected again and again in blues, in *Worried Blues, Thinkin'* and *Worryin'* and *Feel So Bad* by Lightnin' Hopkins, in *Moaning Blues* and *Worried Life Blues* by John Lee Hooker, in *Trouble In Mind* and *Worry Worry* by B.B. King. The 'hurt deep down' is the feeling in blues. It is the cost of having to live under and adapt to the Jim Crow system, of 'living with the blues'.

We can now explain how blues functions in relation to the system. Blues deals with results rather than causes. It articulates the feelings produced by the system. Referring back to the section which analysed the psychological functions of blues, we noted its primary function was cathartic. Blues releases the pain and so soothes and relieves the wounds produced by the system. By 'giving relief', by 'kinda helping somehow' blues helps to make the system bearable to live under.

We may now approach the question of why there is no protest against Jim Crow in blues. At least in recorded material, self-censorship by the singer or censorship by the recording companies would prevent this. However, blues singers state that protest against the system has never been a part of blues. Live performances before black audiences support their claims. Comedians featured on the bill with blues singers at the Regal Theatre condemn racial discrimination with many of their jokes, but there is no hint of protest in the blues sung at the same show. As noted in Chapter 1 the rise and fall in the popularity of blues paralleled the rise and fall of Jim Crow. The reason why there is no protest in blues is a part of the very reason why blues originated and developed. Were Jim Crow less pervasive and powerful, less effective in conditioning those who lived under it, it is probable that blues would never have existed, and a very different form of music with different sentiments would have developed. It was the very helplessness of many black Americans to do anything about their situation that resulted in the creation of blues. Unable to effect change, blacks were forces to live with the situation and the feelings it produced. Blues developed to express and relieve those feelings. Far from opposing the Jim Crow system, blues harmonises with it.

Accommodation and Acceptance in Blues

For the better part of this century, black Americans have been forced to accept a position and a status defined for them and imposed upon them by the wider society. They have been forced to adapt to this situation. B.B. King refers to the partial success of that adaptation: '. . . after you live under that system for so long then it don't bother you openly.' Reggie

Lavong (WWRL) describes the compromise demanded by the system, and the creative response to it.

> If you live in certain circumstances, you are forced for the sake of survival to interpret things in a mind-pleasing way, in order to keep your sanity. Necessity is the mother of invention; you learn to make things more palatable to you. You must make adjustments psychologically, economically, physically, any conceivable way, you must make adjustments.

Blues contains many recipes for compromise. In 1928 Ishman Bracey sings in *Trouble-Hearted Blues,*

> Down so long,
> Down don't worry me,
> I've been down so long, now,
> Down don't worry me.

In 1960 J.B. Lenoir sings,

> I been down so long,
> That being down do not worry me,
> I'm goin' pack my suitcase,
> An' cross the way you know, I'll go.

(Oliver 1965: 146)

In 1968 Albert King sings,

> I've been down so long,
> That down don't bother me,
> I'm gonna take all my troubles,
> And throw them in the deep blue sea.

Reflected and proposed in these songs is an attitude and a strategy for survival. The situation is defined, it is more or less immutable, so nothing can be done about it other than accept it and learn to live with it. Acceptance is the first element in this strategy; making the best of it by attempting to transcend the situation philosphically is the second. Son House illustrates the relationship of the above songs and the strategy they present, with the life of black sharecroppers in Louisiana.

> Some of those that grew crops—if they paid their debts for the food they ate during the year, why if they came out and cleared as much as forty or fifty dollars for a year, they were satisfied. Out of a whole year's work! Of course, along then, they didn't see into it too much because they'd been used to it for so long. They didn't worry over it because they always knew if they didn't have the money, they was still going to eat and have a place to stay, such as it was. So they didn't complain and worry too much about it. (Charters 1967: 59)

For many blacks in the sprawling urban ghettoes with high unemployment rates and substandard housing, a similar adaptation was necessitated. Ed

Cook (WVON) explains the relationship of survival, acceptance and blues from his perspective in Chicago.

> Why do people enjoy songs about troubles. That's the way it is for people who live rough, who have experienced a rough time. It's like laughing at yourself and living with it. We know what it's like to be ostracised by society. We know what it is not to be able to get a job. It's not hard like if I became rich tomorrow and then next week lost everything I had. It wouldn't upset me emotionally like it would some people, because I've been poor before. That's the way it is with us. This is the only way we can continue to exist.

As Ed Cook notes, a further aspect in the strategy of acceptance and philosphical transcendance is humour, irony and self-deprecation. 'Got to laugh to keep from crying' is a recurrent theme in blues. Paul Oliver notes the presence of self-deprecation in blues, and its relation to acceptance: 'He accepts his position in the social sub-stratum . . . in numerous self-abasing metaphors and then rejoices in them: "I'm ragged but right"; "it's dirty but good"; "I'm blue, black and evil but I did not make myself".' (Oliver 1968: 254).

The emphasis in blues is not on changing the situation but on living with it. Adaptation to the status quo rather than improving it is advocated. Blues depicts what life is, rather than what it could or should be. Related to the attitude and strategy of acceptance is a stance of passivity, of doing nothing in the face of problem situations, of submitting to the inevitable. The very act of singing blues is a response to the inability to effect change and improvement. It is, in one sense, an admission of helplessness. Robert Curtis Smith illustrates this point,

> Half the time hungry, and when you get the blues on top of that and you get to thinkin' about where you can go, or what you can do for to change. That's when the blues gets you. When there's nothin' else to do but what you doin' . . . and sing the blues. (Oliver 1965: 2)

Jimmy Rogers recalls the necessity of accepting the situation as it was, and the function of blues in relation to this adaptation,

> You see the older blues men had to live a rough, hard life. Go without a lot of things that he really needs, not want. React to people mistreating you even though there was nothing you could do about it at that time . . . You had to have something to consolidate you, and that was the blues. (*Melody Maker* 18 November 1972: 34).

The recognition that passivity is the only response available to many situations is reflected in blues. In *Worry, Worry* B.B. King admits,

> Oh, worry, worry, worry,
> Worry's all I can do.

The long-time inability of black Americans to act against Jim Crow and improve their status leaves few alternatives other than worrying and crying about the situation, and attempting to struggle on in terms of it, responses that are reflected in blues, feelings that are relieved by blues.

Directly related to passivity is the concept of luck, which is used as an explanation of causation in many blues songs. An individual has little control over his own destiny, which is directed by the vagaries of fate rather than by his own actions. Success and failure are defined as a function of luck rather than effort. In *Bad Luck And Trouble* Boogie Jake sings,

> I don't know why, I don't know why,
> Bad luck and trouble follow me,
> I've tried to be a good boy,
> Fill my life with misery.

Having been 'born under a bad sign', Albert King's fate is predetermined. He sings,

> If it wasn't for bad luck,
> You know I wouldn't have no luck at all.

Having defined causation in terms of luck which cannot be controlled by natural means, supernatural agencies are needed to influence the situation. Blues songs abound in mojos, black cat bones, roots, John the Conquerors, charms and potions to influence fate, remedy bad luck and remove jinxes. In *Mojo Hand*, Lightnin' Hopkins hopes to ensure his woman's faithfulness:

> I'm going to Louisiana,
> And get me a mojo hand,
> I'm gonna fix my woman so,
> She can't have no other man.

Since luck is beyond normal manipulation an attitude of passive acceptance to what fate brings and of inactivity to effect what it will bring is encouraged. This element of fatalism is present in many blues.

When blues does propose positive action it is usually to vacate the scene of the problem rather than resolve it directly. Leaving town is a remedy advocated in a number of blues. In *Feelin' Awful Blues* Lightnin' Slim sings,

> I woke up early this morning,
> I was feeling awful blue,
> Well I felt so bad baby,
> Till I did not know what to do.
>
> I walked down to the station,
> I feel down on my knees,
> I had to catch me a freight train, baby,
> Just to give my poor heart ease.

Escape to Chicago, and occasionally back south again, is a solution suggested in several blues. Putting his faith in luck, Arthur Crudup advocates both routes. In *Chicago Blues* he hopes someday, with luck, to make Chicago his home. However, in *If I Get Lucky* he has second thoughts:

> If I get lucky mama.
> Win my train fare home,
> I'm goin' back to Mississippi,
> Lord now, where I belong.

Blues as a Definition of the Situation

Blues expresses a mood, advocates a strategy and it also defines a situation, it presents a picture of what life is like. The world of blues is a 'mean old world', a 'world full of trouble'. Against a background of black nights and midnight hours, time travels slowly, 'minutes seem like hours and hours seem like days'. Life is hard and unrewarding. The blues singer rarely has 'a cent to pay the rent'. His relationships with women are usually unsuccessful. He either sits alone, unloved and 'blue and lonesome', or worries about his woman with her 'back door friend'. His footsteps are dogged with bad luck and trouble. Few comforting fantasies exist in this world of harsh reality. The sun might be shining but 'it's raining in my heart'.

Blues does not present a mirror image of black society nor an exhaustive catalogue of black culture. A particular view of the world is presented. The picture is selective. It holds forth few promises, portrays few images of a better way of life. In fact it concentrates on many of the harsher aspects of life as it exists. This selective view has important consequences. By defining life as hard and unrewarding and, by implication, the future as the same, blues tends to maintain aspirations and expectations at a low level. It prepares its audience for the future. The expectation of hardship cushions the experience and preconditions people to accept it.

In providing a definition of the situation, blues also provides a rationale for that situation. In answer to the question 'Why do I have hard luck and trouble?' blues replies 'Because life's like that'. Using the concept of 'the blues', songs name and broadcast the state of mind and the way of life. Like many other singers, Buddy Guy in *First Time I Met The Blues* describes his relationship with 'the blues'. After relentlessly pursuing him, 'Mr Blues' becomes his constant companion, morning, noon and night. 'Mr Blues' is a central character in the world portrayed in blues, his presence pervades the life and thoughts of the singer. Little Milton talks about the inevitability of having 'the blues': 'The blues is right there and you're gonna get them.' Big Bill Broonzy notes their indivisibility from life itself: 'Blues is a natural fact, something that a fellow lives' (Courlander 1963: 124). Albert King talks to his audience as he plays a guitar solo,

> Everybody have the blues. You take the little baby that's layin' in the cradle and the bottle ain't comin' fast enough, he got the blues. And I ain't lyin'. Everybody have the blues.

From the cradle to the grave, 'blues is a natural fact'. Life, to quote an oft-recorded song, is 'living with the blues'. This definition of the situation explains life, creates expectations, moulds aspirations and presents and promotes a world view.

The aspects of blues analysed above all support the traditional status of blacks in America. The hurt produced by the system is assuaged and syphoned off in song rather than being turned against it. The frustration produced by the inability to act against the system and to change one's ascribed status is released in blues. A strategy of living with the situation, of accepting one's position and making the best of it, is advocated. Initiative is discouraged and taking what comes encouraged. Blame for one's situation is focussed on luck rather than the system. Expectations and aspirations are contained within the framework of the status quo and so blunted from initiating future change. There are few images of a way of life that differs from the ascribed black role and so standards of comparison which might produce dissatisfaction are lacking. The inevitability and omnipresence of 'blues as a natural fact' imply that it is part of the natural order of things, which negates change, discourages efforts for improvement and promotes accommodation to the status quo. Blues therefore functions within the system to maintain the status of black Americans, and to make that status, if not desirable, at least bearable.

Moving Past the Blues

In the preceding sections, certain aspects of blues have been emphasised. These aspects have been selected because they in particular have led to the present demise of blues. Our major thesis is that the mood and conditions of black Americans have changed to a degree where blues is no longer in accord with them. A change in the themes of blues would fail to bring it into harmony with the present because the meaning and associations are as much within the music as the words themselves. Blues has become an anachronism, a perspective clearly voiced by Jerry B. (WWRL). 'How many people can say honestly that they can identify with blues. Not many. It's like another phase of one's life. Like we're adolescent, then we grow up into adulthood and the blues was like the infant stage.'

The economic conditions which in part gave rise to and sustained blues have changed. 'No food on my table and no shoes on my feet' from John Lee Hooker's *No Shoes* has little meaning for many blacks today. Enoch Gregory (WWRL) explains this aspect of the decline of blues.

> Blues is a music that belong to the downtrodden, those who don't have much to look forward to. But times are changing. Now we have very few people who have not had a meal today. Picking cotton is almost extinct. There's a television set in every house practically. Times generally, in terms of getting the basic necessities of life, are a lot better.

Fred Goree (WCHB) adds, 'It's not the same kind of starvation and abject poverty that the old blues singers went through.' Muddy Waters concludes, 'Ain't got them kind of blues today. The colored ain't. The black people ain't got it today. Eat every day. Eat good.' (*Downbeat* 7 August 1969: 32).

Similarly, with the decline of Jim Crow, blues are out of accord with today's racial situation. Fred Goree (WCHB) states, 'The kids today aren't going through the same kind of blues thing. They're in a different bag. It's not the same kind of racial thing.' Butterball Jr. (WCHB) says, 'In the old days they were really in a blues bag. "The Man" was treatin' him so bad that he had to sing the blues, but it's not like that anymore so they don't have a leg to stand on. The blues singer doesn't have anything to moan about.' Blues no longer has a situation to respond to.

A change in economic conditions and race relations is accompanied by a change in mood. Again, blues is out of harmony with this mood. Hal Atkins (WWRL) says, 'People are tired of being sad, of having the same thing warmed over, "My baby left me" and that kind of thing. You listen to the blues and it's just like hearing the same tune all day.' Butterball (WVON) adds, 'Years ago people identified with all this sadness, all sadness. Now they wanna hear a happy song. They don't wanna hear about some guy who got hit over the head with an axe.'

In line with these changes is a different strategy of adaptation to the situation. Acceptance and accommodation are losing ground. Jerry B. (WWRL) explains this new approach to the present and the future:

> Back then life was a struggle, but there was nothing they could do about it so they may as well accept it. Like 'I've been down so long that down don't bother me', times are hard but I'll accept it 'cos there's nothing else. Now down does bother me and I won't accept it.

Ray Henderson (WCHB) summarises this approach: 'Now they say "Hey, I'm not gonna be down, I gonna get up".' Big Bill Broonzy gives a blues singer's perspective. 'Young people have forgotten how to cry the blues. Now they talk and get lawyers' (Bruynoghe 1964: 17). Feelings formerly turned inward and released in blues are now turned outward and directed toward change.

This strategy is related to a concomitant change in expectations and aspirations, which is antithetical to the message of blues. Hal Atkins (WWRL) explains the relationship between music and aspirations.

Blues is just primarily an experience that you or I had and we're relating that particular experience with no particular outlook for the future. We just become absorbed in a particular experience and buy into a sort of sadistic element . . . The hope of a new day is the thing now so that's why there's no blues.

Enoch Gregory (WWRL) emphasises expectations and hopes for a better future.

It's an age group today that knows something about hope, which knows something about a future. O.K. so I live in a ghetto, but I'm gonna get out of this ghetto and man, I'm gonna make it. So don't play me nothing about molasses and cornbread. I don't wanna know.

New strategies and attitudes, expectations and aspirations have to compete with old ones. Change not only brings a disinterest in past adaptations but often a conscious rejection of them. This process is at work in the response to blues. Bill Williams (WCHB) states, 'Most people who are rejecting blues are definitely trying to throw away old clothes.' Butterball Jr. (WCHB) adds, 'You try and push it [blues] out of your life.' John Lee Hooker gives a blues singer's viewpoint: 'A lot of them don't want to accept it, will not accept it. They think it's a hangover.' Jay Butler (WCHB) presents the view of many young blacks.

The young black American has been trying to get away from what the blues says. He doesn't feel the same thing. He doesn't associate himself with blues music because it doesn't fit his way of life. So you don't get young blues singers coming up anymore.

Times have changed and, to quote Reggie Lavong (WWRL), 'Muddy Waters and Howling Wolf are products of their time.' Blues in black America is inextricably interwoven with black society and culture. When factors within this framework change, the music changes. As new factors emerge so does new music. Blues remains today, to quote John Lee Hooker, as 'a hangover'. Lee Garrett (WGPR) summarises the process: 'As the times changed, the mood of the people changes so this is why blues doesn't make it.'

Changing With The Times

Those still financially and aesthetically committed to blues attempt to drum up support for the music and defend it against its critics. On the reverse of B.B. King's publicity photograph is printed, 'They've got an ol' sayin' "If you don't dig it, don't knock it".' T.V. Slim went as far as to make a record entitled *Don't Knock The Blues*. Pervis Spann and E. Rodney Jones of WVON, who promote most of the big blues shows in Chicago, voice their support for the music in no uncertain terms over the air. Pervis Spann, 'The Blues Man', is well known for his saying, 'If you don't like the blues you've got a hole in your soul.' E. Rodney Jones draws his favourite comparison of B.B. King with Sea Biscuit, a champion

Left: *Little Sonny*. Above: *the WVON disc-jockeys E. Rodney Jones* (right) *and Pervis Spann.*

racehorse. Introducing *The Woman I Love* he says, 'Here's B.B. singing about the woman he loves. We call him the boss hoss 'cos he's just like Sea Biscuit, honey, never lost a race.' Jack Harris of KUXL, Minneapolis, makes his feelings about blues and those who don't like them perfectly clear as he introduces Lowell Fulsom's *Blues Pain:* 'If you don't like the blues you've got no soul. Don't tell me you're too proud because if you don't like blues you're not proud at all and that's bad.' He stays with his theme after the record: 'If you don't like that record you need to go to a witch and have the spell taken off you 'cos there's something wrong.' However, such spirited defences fall mainly on deaf ears.

Blues singers may have an emotional commitment to their music but their main concern is to make a living. They have to change with the times if they can. Evidence from Detroit suggests that local blues singers either update their music or don't work. Little Sonny is the only fully professional blues singer in Detroit and is generally recognised as the most popular locally based singer in that style. Despite his excellent blues harmonica playing and his affirmation of blues with shouts of 'If you got the blues you can't lose', less than a quarter of the songs he sings are blues. Most of his act is made up of soul music and he features songs such as Eddie Floyd's *Knock On Wood* and Aretha Franklin's *Chain of Fools.* Most of the blues he plays, such as *My Babe*, are uptempo with a soul rhythm. Even slow numbers such as *Down Don't Bother Me* are speeded up and backed by a soul beat. Eddie Burns, another local Detroit blues singer, features hardly any blues in his act. Despite being a fine harmonica-player he has dropped that instrument because it doesn't suit his present style. With himself on guitar he leads a hard-driving little band which includes tenor sax, bass and drums. His act consists mainly of soul music and he features such songs as James Brown's *I Feel Good*. The songs that come closest to blues in his act are Bobby Bland's *Turn On Your Lovelight* and Roscoe Gordon's *Just A Little Bit*. Eddie Burns says he used to play a lot of blues but 'I don't play blues much now. Got to change with the times.' He is unable to make a living out of music and in 1968 has a full-time day job. Other local Detroit blues singers such as Washboard Willie, whose style is distinctly archaic, and Mr Bo were not even performing in public during the author's four-week stay in Detroit in 1968.

An evening with J.B. Hutto at Turner's on Chicago's South Side in 1966 shows the penalties of not changing with the times. Hutto's act consists of traditional Chicago Delta-based blues. Even his uptempo numbers are undeniably blues. He plays bottleneck guitar and is backed by two other guitars. Despite the high quality of his performance the bar is half empty and few customers are showing much interest in the music. Even when he is joined later in the evening by Walter Horton on harmonica and they play some superb downhome Chicago blues, only a dozen or so customers show any enthusiasm. Five years later, according to Alex Cramer, J.B. Hutto is still persevering with this same style and having the same lack of success, scraping by on $15 a booking (Cramer 1971: 7). However, his fellow Chicago blues singer, Mighty Joe Young, has compromised with public tastes and is much more successful. Young states, 'Blues is a business, like anything else,' and goes on to say, 'I play a lot of different clubs and I have to play rhythm'n' blues and the Top Ten. You have to mix it up, else they'll walk out on you and go to some other club. Blues has changed a lot. They brought it up with the big beat' (Cramer 1971: 5).

Like their locally based counterparts, the more famous blues singers try to accommodate the changing tastes of the black public. One solution is to leave it to the band. At the Cozy Bar, Minneapolis, Muddy Waters' band performs for most of the evening, playing instrumental versions of songs like *Ode To Billy Joe* and featuring band members singing soul songs made famous by Wilson Pickett and James Brown. Muddy Waters sings only five numbers and draws little more response than his band. On record he has attempted to reach a wider public with songs like *Muddy Waters Twist* and *You Need Love*, the latter sounding like an attempt to recreate Dale Hawkins's rock'n'roll hit *Susie-Q*. Neither record sold well and Muddy Waters has been unable to change his style sufficiently to appeal to a non-blues audience. Junior Parker also tried to broaden his appeal. At the Regal he introduces *Your Love's All Over Me,* an uptempo soul song, with

Right: *J.B. Hutto.*

the words, 'Like to do my latest record. This is for the younger people.' The scattering of younger people in the audience are presented with the incongruous spectacle of a rather stout, middle-aged Mr Parker performing an outdated but very dignified version of the twist as he sings his new song. After 13 years with Duke Records, Junior Parker moved to Mercury and explains his new policy:

> We're trying a new bag. I never did any funky blues with Mercury like I did with Duke. I now do things more for the younger set. I'm tryin' something. If it don't work out then I go back to the old-timers. But I can't feel this rock and roll stuff man. But I gotta keep eating see, so that's why I sing it. So I'm compelled to sing it. Now the backsides of my records, the slow ones, well those are the ones I feel.

Bobby Bland tells a similar story: 'I love the feeling of the blues but what we've turned to now is more or less a beat. You have to change with the trend. Things will never stay the same as they were.' Known for years as Bobby 'Blue' Bland, he is now advertised as Bobby Bland, 'The Soul Man'. His career has been marked by a number of attempts to reach a wider audience. He tried to 'go pop' with songs like *Call On Me* and *That's The Way Love Is* and songs such as *Turn On Your Lovelight* and *Yield Not To Temptation* show a strong gospel influence. Like Junior Parker's, the 'B' sides of Bobby Bland's records are often slow blues.

Even B.B. King, the 'King of the Blues', has had to fight hard to maintain the integrity of his style. He recalls the dangers of being booked to appear with rock 'n' roll groups in the late '50s.

> I was billed with rock and roll groups. They were dancing all over the stage and I didn't do that. When I was up there it was B.B. King alone. I had to work extra hard and fast to keep from being booed. It really hurt. After all these years you say to yourself 'Somebody must like me.' (*Newsweek* 26 May 1969: 84)

B.B. had a short flirtation with pop music in the early '60s, though the songs were confined to records rather than personal appearances. Recordings such as *Young Dreamers* and *On My Word Of Honor*, sentimental ballads with lush string sections and girl choirs singing pop harmonies, were a short-lived experiment.

Only a couple of singers who first recorded and established themselves as blues artists have managed to reach a large black public with a change of style. Junior Wells and Little Milton are now able to adapt to either blues or soul audiences. Junior Wells records blues LPs for Vanguard which sell to a largely white audience, and soul music for Blue Rock (a subsidiary of Mercury) mainly for a black audience. He had minor hits in northern ghettoes with his soul singles *Up In Heah* and *You're Tuff Enough*. Little Milton has moved steadily away from blues towards soul music. Since his

Left: *Mighty Joe Young.*

album 'Little Milton Sings Big Blues', released in 1966, he has rarely recorded blues. Most blues singers are too tied to their style to emulate Junior Wells and Little Milton successfully. Age is probably a factor, as these two singers are among the youngest blues singers. The majority follows the pattern of the aging and uncompromising Howling Wolf when they attempt to move away from blues. Venturing into the soul market, he covered Syl Johnson's *Sock It To Me*, which he modestly retitled *Pop It To Me*. His effort met with a singular lack of financial reward, his style being too personal and inflexible to sound anything other than Howling Wolf the blues singer trying unsuccessfully to sing soul music.

Blues and Whites

As late as the summer of 1968, B.B. King said rather uncertainly, 'I'm gonna try and see if the white people will dig what I have to offer.' Later that same year he played the Fillmore West, and says of that performance,

> The last time we played there it was 95% black in 1963. This time it was 95% white. I was shocked. Mike Bloomfield introduced me as the greatest bluesman. I didn't know if I could walk out there. When I finally did they gave me a standing ovation. I wanted to cry. Words can't say how I felt. (*Newsweek* 26 May 1969: 84)

B.B. King and other blues singers are now reaping the financial and aesthetic rewards of large white audiences. Albert King, a favourite at the Fillmores East and West before they were closed in 1971, prefers playing before a white audience because he can develop his music, and doesn't have to play solely 'old time stuff' to traditionally oriented nostalgic black audiences at venues like the Regal. Muddy Waters appreciates white audiences for the opposite reason; they enjoy his traditional downhome Chicago blues. 'The blacks are more interested in the jumpy stuff. The whites want to hear me for what I am' (*Time,* 9 August 1971: 41). B.B. King's reasons are similar. The Regal is one of the few places he can play blues the way he likes before a large black audience and still be accepted and enjoyed. B.B. King's comparison of his reception by a white audience at the Cafe au Go-Go to that by a black audience at Harlem's Apollo Theatre is illuminating.

> They [the white audience] knew about the blues before I came there—they was wantin' to listen to what we had to offer. The Apollo was different. The Apollo was listenin' to everything that was comin' in—to see what you had. They wasn't particularly interested, well, I'd say 60% wasn't, to just what we are doin'. But the Go-Go, they were interested in what I had to offer, and they came to listen, not dance, not clap their hands, or do anything of this sort, but listen. The Apollo they want to see what you look like—I'll put it in percentage-wise: 60% of what you look like, 30% dancing—they want to see, shall we say the other 10% is actual talent . . . [As for

white audiences] I believe they are understandin' it, and the ones
that are not understandin' it are tryin' to and they are actually tryin'
to be a part of what's goin' on. I hardly know how to put this but
they are sincere. (*Soul Sounds* 31 October 1968: 6)

John Lee Hooker echoes these views. He appreciates white audiences after
the apathy and occasional barracking he receives from black audiences:
'The whites, they really appreciates the blues, they really gets with it
y'know, they really sincere, it's no come on, it's no gimme, it's no put on,
they for real y'know, and it can make you feel real good. I just can't
believe they dig it so deep.'

B.B. King, Albert King, Muddy Waters, John Lee Hooker and Lightnin'
Hopkins now play the lucrative, largely white, college and university
venues across America. B.B. King is particularly popular and appears
regularly on nationally networked TV shows. Yet as late as May 1969 he
stated, 'I've never been asked to appear at a black college.' Albert King
sums up the financial rewards of the new-found white audience: 'My days
of paying dues are over. Now it's my turn to do the collecting' (*Newsweek*
26 May 1969: 85). However, at the time of this research the important
talents of less traditional blues singers such as Bobby Bland, Junior Parker
and Little Milton seem to have eluded the young white American middle
classes in their search for authenticity and meaning. (While this book was
being written, Junior Parker's tragic death on 18 November 1971, was
reported. He never achieved the success his talents deserved with a white
audience. The title of his last LP, 'You Don't Have To Be Black To Love
The Blues', shows he was still trying to break through to that audience.)

The reasons for white support for blues singers do not concern us in
this book. What does is that many blues singers are being priced out of
many black venues, especially the smaller clubs and bars where blues is
seen at its best. Since their new-found success their fees have risen steeply.
As B.B. King says, 'If I played some of the places I used to play, well,
nobody would get paid really. Because a lot of the places couldn't afford
to pay what we need to survive' (*Melody Maker* 1 May 1971: 35). This
situation had led to the place of blues in black society growing even
smaller. Most blues singers now look to a white audience. Otis Rush plays
the white clubs like Alice's Restaurant on Chicago's hippy/tourist North
Side. He prefers to play there, 'The money's better in the white clubs and
the black joints are rough' (*Melody Maker* 2 October 1971: 30). If the
present trend continues the white North Side rather than the black South
and West Sides will be the place to hear blues in Chicago and blues singers
will lose what few connections they retain within the black community.

Over page: *from ghetto bars to concert halls—Albert King with the St
Louis Symphony Orchestra.*

Conclusion

Despite the minority support for blues in black America, all indications point to its extinction as a black musical form. Singers are middle-aged and older, and there are few younger men to take their place. Audiences are also advanced in years and show no sign of changing. Blues has meant too much and still means too much to blacks for them to follow the fashions of white America. The present is in soul music and all indications suggest the future is there too.

3/Moving On Up

Soul Music and Black Radio

Three o'clock, Saturday afternoon, 22 June 1968, 'Butterball and WVON present another hour of soul power' blares from radios across Chicago's South and West Side ghettoes.

> Let's make it heart rockin' and soul sockin'. Super soul, soul power, hit number four. Let's do it to it,

shouts Butterball, bouncing up and down on his cushion, sweat trickling down his temples, and *The Horse* by Cliff Nobles blasts forth.

The sound is the same in black ghettoes across America. The broadcasting format of black radio varies little from station to station. Chicago's WVON broadcasts rather more gospel music than most, but in other respects is typical. The day starts at 4.30 am with gospel and spiritual music. This is followed from 6.00 am to 11.00 pm with 17 hours of soul music interspersed with the occasional blues number. From 11.00 pm till 12.00 midnight, 'The Hot Line' presents topics on local and national issues of particular interest to the black audience. Soul music returns until 4.30 am. Sunday is devoted to gospel music and live broadcasts from local churches are featured. Like most stations WVON is white-owned. In 1968 less than ten of the stations aimed at black audiences were black-owned. However, the programme directors and disc-jockeys, the people who choose and play the records, are almost invariably black. As a general rule the money is white but the voices are black.

To assess the relative popularity of various styles of secular music, surveys of the records played over three-week periods during the summer of 1968 were taken for WVON, Chicago, WCHB, Detroit and WWRL, New York. These stations have the largest shares of the black audience in their respective cities. The survey results show the percentage of soul music played was 91.8 for WVON, 96.2 for WCHB and 93.2 for WWRL. (Percentages are based on the number of different records played, and do not take into account the relative frequency with which they were played.) A similar picture emerges from shorter surveys from other black stations in these same cities, e.g. 97.4% for WBEE, Chicago and 91.2% for WJLB, Detroit. Evidence from radio stations in other northern towns and cities is similar, e.g. 92.5% for WMPP, East Chicago and Gary, Indiana (July-August 1967), and 93.1% for KUXL, Minneapolis (June-July 1969). As noted in Chapter 1, the percentages for soul music would be even higher had not a broad definition of blues been adopted.

Clearly black audiences in these cities prefer soul to other forms of music. The extent of this preference may be seen from the size of the black radio audience and its commitment to black stations. An independent survey states that 'WVON named "favorite station" by 64% of Chicago Negro households—more than double the percentage of the next four stations combined', and that 'WVON reaches 90% of all Chicago Negro households every week' (*Ignore it and Lose* 1968: 7). Turning to Detroit, Figure 1 gives estimates for the number of black households there tuned to particular radio stations.

Figure 1

Number of Black Households in Detroit Reached In Average Quarter-hour periods over a Five-day Week

RADIO STATION	6-10 a.m.	10-3 p.m.	3-7 p.m.	7 p.m.-12 MIDNIGHT
CKLW	2,400	2,560	2,880	960
WCHB	25,550	20,920	38,490	13,900
WCHD-FM	800	4,150	5,750	3,510
WGPR-FM	3,350	2,080	3,040	1,280
WJLB	11,180	9,740	11,340	3,350
WJR	2,400	1,440	2,400	800
Misc.	6,550	5,270	6,070	2,240
Total	52,230	46,160	69,970	26,040

Note: Adapted from The Pulse, Inc., Detroit City Michigan Negro Audience, February-March 1968:6-7.

Directly comparable data for other cities were unobtainable. The percentage share of each radio station of the total black audience in Detroit and New York is given in Figure 2. The cities' main soul stations, WCHB and WWRL, are by far the most popular.

The commitment of black audiences to black radio in general and soul music in particular becomes clearer by examining the broadcasting formats of the stations that figure in the Detroit and New York surveys. They are summarised in Figure 3. The only stations aiming at a specifically black audience, which do not broadcast soul music, play jazz, mainly 'soul-jazz' of the Jimmy Smith, Jimmy McGriff, Brother Jack McDuff variety. These stations have a faithful but minority following within the black audience.

The 'Top 40' refers to the best selling records in the United States based on charts in trade publications such as *Billboard* and *Record World*. Top 40 stations stick fairly closely to these charts. It is important to note that these stations, which have a small percentage of the black audience (significantly larger in New York, however, compared with Chicago and Detroit), do play a number of soul records. A three-week survey of the

Figure 2

Percentage Share of Each Radio Station of the Total Black Audience Reached at Least once a Week by Stations in Detroit and New York

DETROIT		NEW YORK	
Station	*Percentage of Weekly Audience*	*Station*	*Percentage of Weekly Audience*
CKLW	11.0	WABC	15.6
WCHB	65.4	WABC-FM	1.2
WCHD-FM	17.6	WCBS	9.9
WGPR-FM	9.8	WINS	24.6
WJLB	37.7	WLIB	18.5
WJR	5.0	WLIB-FM	7.0
All stations	100.0	WMCA	16.2
		WNBC	8.1
		WNEW	6.3
		WNEW-FM	1.9
		WNJR	8.4
		WOR	15.1
		WWRL	45.0
		All stations	100.0

Note: Adapted from The Pulse, Inc. Detroit Michigan Negro Audience, February-March 1968:4.

Note: Adapted from *The Pulse, Inc.,* New York City Five County Survey Area, Negro Radio Audience, January-April 1968:5.

Figure 3

Broadcasting Format of Radio Stations in Detroit and New York

DETROIT

Station	*Style of Programmes*
CKLW	Top 40, soul music.
WCHB	Soul music
WCHD-FM	Jazz, mainly black instrumentalists
WGPR	Soul music, plus foreign language programs
WJLB	Soul music plus foreign language programs.

NEW YORK

Station	*Style of Programs*
WABC	Top 40
WABC-FM	'Middle of the road' music, instrumentals
WCBS	All news format
WINS	All News Format
WLIB	Soul music
WLIB-FM	Jazz, mainly black instrumentalists
WMCA	Top 40
WNBC	'Middle of the road' music, talk/conversation
WNEW	'Middle of the road' music
WNEW-FM	Progressive jazz
WNJR (New Jersey)	Soul music
WOR	News, talk/conversation
WWRL	Soul music

national charts of best selling records in *Record World* shows 15, 13 and 16 soul records respectively for the weeks beginning 10, 17 and 24 August 1968 in the Top 40. (*Record World* 23: 1105 [1968] 30; 1106 [1968] 95; 1107 [1968] 25.)

As noted in Chapter 1, radio stations give a reasonable indication of black musical tastes. Radio offers a wide range of music. It is the easiest possible context in which to exercise freedom of choice, involving as it does minimal effort. It is extremely doubtful whether any form of music which had a strong minority following within the black audience would be unrepresented on radio. Stations are in contact with the record-buying habits of their audiences, as they receive weekly returns from selected record shops. The industry is highly competitive, with more than one station aimed at the same ethnic group in the larger cities.

Soul Music

Soul music is predominantly vocal and almost all the singers are black. The three-week surveys show that WVON played 61 records, 56 by black vocalists, 3 by black instrumentalists and 2 by non-black vocalists; WCHB, 52 records all by black vocalists: WWRL, 73 records, 64 by black vocalists, 4 by black instrumentalists and 5 by non-black vocalists. Only WVON keeps details of its past 'play lists' from which most of the records played are selected. During 1967 its 'play lists' contained 774 vocal records and all but 10 of these were by black singers.

Standard musical notation fails to distinguish between soul and other forms of music. A formal code based on different concepts would have to be devised to make the distinction. However, blacks are in no doubt that such a distinction exists. They often make the point that most white artists performing a soul song may achieve an accurate copy of a black original in terms of strict musical notation, but the final product lacks the overall sound, quality and feeling of soul music. There are rare exceptions of white artists making records in the style of soul music, that are acceptable to a large black audience. *Groovin'* by The Young Rascals and *1-2-3* by Len Barry were played regularly on many black radio stations. As Lucky Cordell (WVON) states, style rather than colour is the criterion on which records are selected.

> We play a sound rather than negroid music . . . our music is primarily by Negro artists. But this is because there are so few white artists that record our sound. Take Len Barry. We played his *1-2-3* but his records after that were not our kind of sound.

Particular songs in themselves cannot be classified as soul or non-soul music. The Beatles' songs as they perform them are not considered to be soul music. However, versions of their songs performed by black soul singers, e.g. *Eleanor Rigby* by Ray Charles, *Ticket to Ride* by Willie Walker

THE SOUL SOUND

WBEE 1570

B E E L I N E · U P

1.	You're My Everything	Tempations
2.	Baby I Love You	Aretha Franklin
3.	Cold Sweat	James Brown
4.	Get On Up	Esquires
5.	Hypnotized	Linda Jones
6.	Don't You Miss Me	Jimmy Ruffin
7.	As Long As I Live	Fantastic Four
8.	Groovin	Booker T & MG's
9.	Karate Boo-ga-loo	Jerry O
10.	Pearl Time	Andrea Williams
11.	Everybody Needs Love	Gladys Knight & Pips
12.	Funky Broadway	Wilson Pickett
13.	Forget It	Sandpebbles
14.	Take Care	June Conquest
15.	Will You Be Ready	Samson & Deliah
16.	Love Is a Doggone Good Thing	Eddie Floyd
17.	Check My Tears	Trends
18.	Get Down	Harvey Scales & 7 Sounds
19.	Higher Higher	Jackie Wilson
20.	You Got To Pay The Price	Al Kent
21.	Last Minute Miracles	Shirelles
22.	Gimme A Little Sign	Brenton Wood
23.	Can't Stop Loving You	Otis Leville
24.	Just Once In a Lifetime	Mike & Censtations
25.	Different Stookes	The Intruders
26.	Someday Baby	Archie Bell & The Drells
27.	I Need You So	The Cruisers
28.	There Goes the Loved	Gene Chandler
29.	Nothing I Can Do About It	Miek & Censtations
30.	A Love That's Real	The Intruders
31.	She's My Woman	Archie Bell & The Drells
32.	I Can't Stay Away From You	Impressions
33.	Eloise	William Bell
34.	Hang Over	Martinis
35.	Under The Street Lamps	The Exits

BEE BREAKER: Do The Skin . . . . Kennard Gardner

CHICAGO TALENT SPOTLIGHT:
  Just Because . . . . Willie Williams

ALBUM OF THE WEEK: "Aretha Arrives" . . Aretha Williams

THE SOUL SOUND

ILL KENNER   ROBERT WEAVER   REV. W.N. DANIEL   VINCE SANDERS   SCOTT GORMAN

WJLB
SUPERADIO 1400
DETROIT

FAST 40 SURVEY

SUPERADIO - 1400 - DETROIT · SUPERADIO - 1400 - DETROIT

SUPERADIO SURVEY—JULY 22, 1968

1. YOU MET YOUR MATCH .... Stevie Wonder (Tamla)
2. ELEANOR RIGBY .... Ray Charles (ABC)
3. I'VE NEVER FOUND A GIRL .... Eddie Floyd (Stax
4. GRAZING IN THE GRASS .... Hugh Masekela (Uni)
5. HANGING ON .... Joe Simon (Sound Stage 7)

6. LOVE IS LIKE A BASEBALL GAME .... Intruders (Gamble)
7. GIRLS CAN'T DO WHAT THE GUYS DO....... Betty Wright (Alston)
8. STONED SOUL PICNIC .... 5th Dimension (Soul City)
9. LOVE MAKES A WOMAN .... Barbara Acklin (Brunswick)
10. GOOD OLD MUSIC .... The Parliaments (Revilot)

11. I'M A MIDNIGHT MOVER .... Wilson Pickett (Atlantic)
12. SEND MY BABY BACK .... Freddie Hughes (Wand)
13. SOUL LIMBO .... Booker T & The M.G.'s (Stax)
14. I LOVED AND I LOST .... The Impressions (ABC)

15. SAVE YOUR LOVE FOR ME .... Bobby Bland (Duke)

16. AIN'T THAT LOVIN' YOU .... The Volumes (Inferno)
17. TAKE ME THE WAY I AM.................. Detroit Emeralds (Ric Tic)
18. DON'T LET HIM TAKE YOUR LOVE FROM ME .. Jimmy Ruffin (Soul)
19. I GUESS I'LL HAVE TO CRY .... James Brown (King)
20. PEOPLE GOT TO BE FREE .... The Rascals (Atlantic)

21. LOVE BUG GOT A BEAR HUG .... Melvin Davis (Mala)
22. WHAT A MAN .... Linda Lyndell (Volt)
23. SOUL MEETING .... Soul Clan (Atlantic)
24. NOTHING SWEETER................................. Eddie Hill (MS)
25. I CAN'T STOP DANCING .... Archie Bell & The Drells (Atlantic)

26. GOD BLESS OUR LOVE .... The Ballads (Venture)
27. YOU MIGHT NEED ME ANOTHER DAY .... Gloria Taylor (King Soul)
28. STAY IN MY CORNER .... The Dells (Cadet)
29. YOU'RE ALL I NEED .... Marvin Gaye/Tammy Terrell (Tamla)
30. HOLD ME TIGHT .... Johnny Nash (J A D Records)

31. THE WOMAN I LOVE .... B. B. King (Kent)
32. OH! .... Jay Lewis (Venture)
33. TOUCH ME .... Chic Carbo (Revue)
34. WOMAN LOVE .... Albert Washington (Fraternity)
35. I THANK YOU KINDLY .... Dianne Lewis (Wand)

Super Chart Challengers

DOWN IN THE DUMPS .... Miriam Makeba (Reprice)
DO THE TIGHTEN UP .... Major Lance (Dakar Records)
THE FUNKY JUDGES .... Bull & The Matadors (Toddlin' Town)
LET'S LET OUR LOVE ROLL ON .... The Magic Tones (Mah's Records)
FUNKY FOUR CORNERS .... Jerryo (Boo-ga-loo)

Super Pick

FLY ME TO THE MOON .... Bobby Womack (Minit)

Super Album

THE MIGHTY MARVELOWS .... The Mighty Marvelows (ABC) and *Day Tripper* by The Vontastics, are classified as soul music. Defining characteristics are to be found in the style of the singer and orchestration rather than in the song itself. In practice soul music is defined by consensus and example. There is little disagreement among black Americans over what is or is not soul music. Definitions are given by example, as in Marvin L. Simms's *Talkin' 'Bout Soul*. He mentions the names of four of the more famous soul singers while the brass section and guitar play extracts from one of their best known songs.

Everybody talkin' 'bout soul,
How it make you feel now,
But I just wanna know baby,
Do they really know the deal now

All you got to do is feel it,
I'm talkin' 'bout soul.

Now if you ask old James,
He can tell you all about it.
[Brass riff and guitar phrase from *Papa's Got a Brand New Bag* by James Brown.]

And Wilson Pickett say
[Brass introduction—with adapted harmony—from *In The Midnight Hour* by Wilson Pickett.]

Memphis sound,
This is the best soul around,
And it kind of does somethin' to you,
When you hear Sam and Dave get down.
[Brass riff and guitar phrase from *Soul Man* by Sam and Dave.]

It's the Same but Different

Little Milton sings the old rhythm and blues favourite *Let The Good Times Roll*. He uses Sam Cooke's arrangement and his singing brings the song even closer to gospel music than Sam Cooke's version. In the middle of the song he shouts to the audience, 'This is the time to get this church thing together. Clap your hands', and the audience claps and sways in unison.

Black singers and disc-jockeys maintain that soul music is a synthesis of gospel music and blues. They see a basic continuity of structure and feeling in all black music, past and present. Bill Williams (WCHB) gives a typical view:

Soul music derives from the gospel thing and the camp meeting thing, the plantation scenes and all the old blues singers who started singing songs of sorrow. Most of these songs had the same feel, the same basic pattern, and the soul music we play today is an outgrowth of these things.

Soul music is probably more closely related to gospel music than to blues. B.B. King gives a blues singer's perspective: 'In James [Brown] 's and Aretha [Franklin] 's case they are more like in church, a Holiness church, where everybody's getting the beat, getting the feeling.' Soul singers often demand the emotional involvement of their audience in much the same way as gospel singers. James Brown exhorts his audience to 'feel good' and 'get the feeling' and directs its mood with songs like *I Feel Good* and *I Got The Feeling*. Like the lead singer in a gospel group he sings 'Hey hey I feel alright' and invites the audience to voice its response. Sam and Dave encourage their listeners to clap along, a feature of gospel music, as they begin *I Thank You* in a singing-preaching style,

I want everybody to get off your seat,
And get your arms together and your hands together,
And give me some of that old soul clappin',
Yeah, a little louder, a little louder, c'mon.

This similarity of response to soul and gospel music may also be seen from radio programmes. Black disc-jockeys punctuate records with shouts of 'C'mon', 'Lord have mercy', 'Good God', 'Do it righteously' and 'Testify, brother, testify'. Ray Henderson (WCHB) explains their derivation. 'They all come from the church. Take "c'mon" . . . the deacon say "c'mon son" if you're singing or if you were testifying. It's an encouraging thing.' Disc-jockeys sometimes testify how soul music makes them feel with emotional monologues that are little different from their religious models. Lee Garrett, 'The Rocking Mr. G' (WGPR), gives a fine performance after *It's A Miracle* by Willie Hightower.

Yeah, I wanna testify, I wanna tell the world how I feel. Oo mercy, I feel so good children, I feel so doggone good. Little Bobby's in the back there shoutin'. He's standin' up with his hands on his head and he say 'Burn baby burn' 'cos I feel good. Aw my goodness, the soul is in me chillun. Lord have mercy! Good God almighty! I say it, I say it, I say it, I say it, it's a miracle what love can do. I know, I know, deep down in my soul I know, deep down in my heart I know, deep down in my bones I know, that it's a miracle.

There is general agreement that soul music began in the mid-'50s when Ray Charles, who had formerly sung blues in a style similar to Charles Brown, began to record secular versions of gospel songs. In 1954 *My Jesus Is All The World To Me* became Ray Charles's *I Got A Woman*. The following year the 'Reverend Mr Ray', the 'High Priest' or the 'Righteous Mr Ray' as he has variously been termed, gave a similar treatment to Clara Ward's old gospel song *This Little Light Of Mine*. Retitling it *This Little Girl Of Mine*, Ray changed a few words to sing the praises of his girlfriend instead of his maker. The traditionally strict separation of blues and religious music was ended. Many, particularly older people, considered the merging of sacred and secular to be in bad taste. The late Big Bill Broonzy, a blues singer, criticised Ray Charles: 'He's got the blues, he's cryin' sanctified. He's mixin' the blues with the spirituals. I know that's wrong . . . he's got a good voice but it's a church voice. He should be singin' in a church' (Karpe n.d.). Black radio stations still receive the occasional complaint from listeners for playing soul songs which are little changed from their gospel originals. Ray Charles however sees the issue in musical rather than moral terms.

> I guess you might say I'm influenced by gospel material. I love a good gospel song if it is really soulful. And if you love something then it's bound to rub off a little . . . Whether blues and gospel or whether it's classical music, there is good and bad. It has to be a fine song and the artist has to feel it or it's no good. (Grevatt n.d.)

Ray Charles' *What'd I Say* is one of the best examples of the amalgam of blues and gospel. Within a twelve-bar blues framework, using a fairly standard blues melody, Ray sings with the emotional techniques of a gospel singer: shouts, screams and broken cries. The brass section responds as a gospel chorus augmented by a vocal trio, the Raelettes. A call-and-response pattern replaces the brass riffs of blues and rhythm and blues, which play counter melodies rather than directly echo the vocal line. In other songs such as *Tell All The World About You*, Ray uses standard gospel chord progressions and gospel piano styling, featuring the Raelettes in a chorus role. James Brown, 'the young man who put soul into rock and roll', exemplifies many of the features of gospel music that have been incorporated into soul. In *Shout And Shimmy* he uses falsetto screams and melisma with wild exuberance and does a parody of testifying at the beginning and during the middle of the song. The emotional preaching style of many black ministers is a device used by several soul singers. (The Reverend C.L. Franklin, Aretha's father, pastor of the New Bethel Baptist Church in Detroit, exemplifies this style. Nurses are regularly on hand to aid members of his congregation overcome by the power and emotion of his presentation.) Solomon Burke employs the style in *Everybody Needs Somebody To Love*, which he begins by delivering his message in the style of a sermon, and offering salvation with the suggestion that if everybody were to sing this song it would save the world.

By the mid-'60s when soul music became the dominant form of black popular music, its style became formalised. The use of the twelve-bar blues framework and blues harmonies declined. There was a greater diversity of chord sequences which gave more opportunity for variation in melody than the rigid twelve-bar blues structure had provided. Gospel chord progressions such as the constant repetition of short chord sequences or the maintenance of a single chord were often employed. Aretha Franklin's

Since You've Been Gone is an example of the former. The song closes with one bar of the tonic and one bar of the subdominant, repeated over and over again. At a live performance this pattern can last well over five minutes with Aretha singing and shouting with increasing fervour and intensity. The pattern is simplified still further by James Brown, who sometimes maintains a single chord for almost the entire song. Free from any change of direction chord progressions might impose, he is able to concentrate on a unidirectional increase in volume, excitement and intensity.

The vocal techniques of many soul singers were learned from apprenticeships in church choirs and amateur and professional gospel groups. At 14, Aretha Franklin was touring with her father's gospel caravan, and with her older sister Erma and two other girls she formed a gospel quartet. She credits her father as her main influence, having sung her first solo in his church at the age of ten. 'Most of what I learned vocally came from him. He gave me a sense of timing in music' (Garland 1969: 199). Like Aretha, James Brown began his career in a gospel group, where, he claims, he learned to scream. Professional gospel groups have produced many soul singers. Sam Cooke, Johnnie Taylor and James Carr all sang at various times with the famous Soul Stirrers. Sometimes an

Left: *Aretha Franklin*. Above: *Ray Charles*.

entire group changes from gospel to soul music, the Sweet Inspirations being a case in point.

However, it is important not to make too much of the gospel background of soul singers. They sing soul music not so much because of this background but rather because there is a demand for the music. Aretha Franklin largely ignored her early experience and began her career in secular music singing jazz and popular standards. Many soul singers began singing some or all of rock 'n' roll, rhythm and blues and blues. Joe Tex sang all three. Otis Redding began by imitating Little Richard's rock 'n' roll style. Johnnie Taylor made some blues records before commiting himself to soul. Clarence Carter and Syl Johnson spent a number of years as blues singers before turning to soul. Singers utilise their gospel training in secular music only when public tastes demand they do so. Many of the more famous blues singers began their singing careers in church choirs or gospel groups. Little Milton and Bobby Bland began in their local church choirs. B.B. King and Junior Parker both sang in gospel quartets while they were at school. However, they all made successful careers as blues singers at a time when this was still possible. It is the popularity of soul music that gives singers the opportunity to employ many of the techniques they used as gospel singers.

The unbroken heritage of black music and the continuity of feeling blacks experience from their music, past and present, may tend to explain why all ages are well represented in radio audiences. The estimated breakdown of the audience for WCHB, Detroit's major soul station is, 26% teens (12-17 years), 36% men and 38% women (The Pulse Inc. (1) 1968: 3) and for WWRL, New York's most popular soul station, 30% teens, 23% men and 47% women (The Pulse Inc. (2) 1968: 14). Butterball (WVON) explains the process of socialisation and the importance of tradition in accounting for the widespread popularity of soul music:

> A lot of the Negro artists were brought up in church. The background of the Negro race as a whole is deeply involved with religion. But this is what you learn from a baby, you've been taught this ever since you were able to understand what the sound is you're hearing. And when you leave that you still have this sound, this rhythm in your mind, like Aretha Franklin when she left . . . In soul music you have this religious sound, you can't get away from it, it's part of you, you were born with it.

Talkin' 'Bout Soul—the Singer

James Brown talks to his audience at the Minneapolis Auditorium, 25 April 1968: 'Yeah, I was just a shoe shine boy and I'm still one of you, I haven't changed. Can you feel it?' James regularly plays to capacity crowds at black theatres across the country: the Apollo, New York, the Howard, Washington D.C., the Regal, Chicago, the Uptown, Philadelphia, the Royal, Baltimore, and many more. The thousands of black Americans who flock to his performances every year all know the story of the poor kid from Augusta, Georgia, who picked cotton, worked as a shoe shine boy and rose from the depths of poverty to become a millionaire and meet the President. James misses few opportunities to tell his fans that he knows what it's like to be black and poor. 'This is one cat that knows the meaning of misery. I've been up and I've been down and I know what DOWN is—it's bad', he writes in his column in *Soul*, a bi-weekly tabloid (*Soul* 3 June 1968: 13).

James Brown personifies the belief that, like the blues singer, the soul singer has experienced what he is singing about. The experience of poverty and hardship and of being black is seen as an essential apprenticeship for the soul singer, and conversely, this experience is seen to be reflected in the music itself. Ed Cook (WVON) states, 'The only way a singer can communicate with his audience is he will have to live it or experience it. For example Ray Charles, he's experienced everything, he's blind, not only that he's Negro, he's been addicted to narcotics, he's lived it all.' The common experience of blackness and poverty and the beliefs which surround the music enables black audiences to relate directly to soul singers. Hal Atkins (WWRL) assesses the importance of James Brown, 'A man like James Brown who has come from grief to glory, he has experienced just about everything that the poor man, the people in the ghetto areas, are experiencing now and he knows how to reach them better than a Dr Martin Luther King.' Despite his success, James Brown is still regarded as one of the people. Lee Garrett (WCPR) states, 'James has still got it. It's a thing of coming from the bottom to the top but never losing that feelin' you had when you were at the bottom.' To retain his success

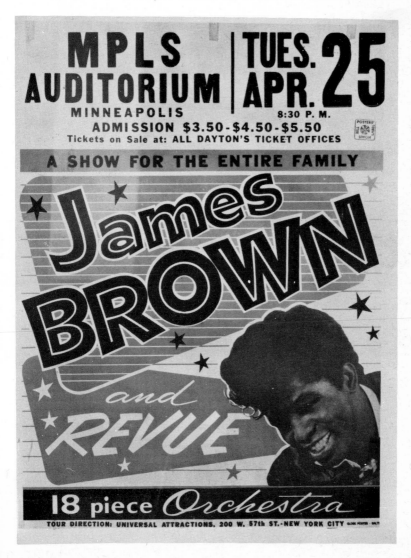

the soul singer must maintain these beliefs. One of the most important ways of doing this is to keep his style. Fred Goree (WCHB) states, 'James Brown is still able to relate because he hasn't changed his style. This shows he hasn't forgotten where he came from.' James has made it as a black man without compromising his style. His songs are full of the hip phraseology of ghetto dialect; in his stage act he performs the latest black dances. Like the blues singer, James Brown is his audience writ large. However, unlike the blues singer, he epitomises, for many members of his audience, the successful black man. His background reflects their past and present, his present their aspirations for the future. Butterball's view illustrates the above points and embroiders the James Brown legend in the process.

> James Brown is a very rich man. He owns several radio stations. He has several jet aircraft and a helicopter [at the time of the interview he owned one Lear jet]. He's a very rich guy after all those hit records he's had but he'll still come out on a stage and work till he's sweaty and I mean really work. This is why they call him Soul Brother Number One. If he's entertaining and he doesn't feel like he's got the message across, even though they applauded for his appearance, he'll run back on stage and do this thing till he can tell the audience feels the message he was tryin' to portray. [James Brown always closes his show with the same ritual. Aides cover his shoulders with a gold lamé cape and support him as he is led, apparently exhausted from the stage. Suddenly he pummels his legs up and down, throws the cape off his shoulders and screams into the microphone, dancing back to the centre of the stage to roars of acclaim. This performance is repeated with a silver cape and finally James clad in a pink cape is led, literally exhausted, from the stage.] This is as soul as soul can be because here's a guy that's made all that money, and where a lot of entertainers tend to get stuff shirtish or phony, no, he's still the same. This is soul. You can meet him on the street and say 'Hey, you got a light' and he say 'Sure, I got a light'. I would venture to say James Brown, if he saw your car stuck in the snow, would help you push it and you would never know he was an entertainer. He's not a phony entertainer.

Associated with the belief that the soul singer sings about his own experiences, experiences which are a product of the conditions he has shared with his audience, is the belief that he is expressing his true and innermost feelings and emotions. In the words of Enoch Gregory (WWRL),

> soul singers get down to the profoundness of their inner self, and bring this up into the tune. It's rare you'll see a live performance done twice the exact same way. This is because the human feeling, the current immediate human feeling has so much to do with this thing called soul, and lines like James Brown saying 'now get to that', it's the mood of the moment.

Singers are seen to live their songs; the songs are seen as a context in which they can express exactly how they feel. Lee Garrett (WGPR)'s statement is representative of the views of many blacks.

> The black man sings from his soul and this is where the term soul music originates. It's more than singing with feeling, it has a little something else. If you take Otis Redding, he not only sang, he cried, and when he was happy, he laughed.

In many ways a singer may be likened to a political representative. His position depends upon the support of the people, they pay his salary and to some extent influence what he has to say. Unlike the politician the singer has no guaranteed term of office, so must constantly give the people what they want to retain his position. This comparison is particularly apt with reference to the black community, which until recently has had little political representation and almost no public voice. Black audiences have largely created the successful soul singer by buying his records and paying to see him. In a very real sense the singer is a chosen representative of the people. The importance of this relationship between singer and public is seen by Lee Garrett (WGPR): 'Soul singers are important because it's someone who is in the light, the public light, someone the public looks up to has touched on their problem, and it makes you smile to know that someone understands your problems.' Jerry B. (WWRL) draws an analogy with and makes a distinction between James Brown and white politicians.

When James Brown says 'Uh with your bad self' [the first line of *Say It Loud*] he acknowledges me, in other words he knows I'm trying to do something. And this is the thing the people in black ghettoes are saying to the white power structure, 'Realise I'm here, realise the problems I have.' James Brown knows the problems we have. The people in Harlem are trying to say to Mayor Lindsay, 'Look at this, come over here and see this man, and do something about it.' And this is the type of feeling I would have when James Brown would say 'Uh with your bad self.' But Mayor Lindsay is not saying 'Uh with your bad self' to these people in Harlem. But James still socks it to 'em even though he's a millionaire and he's got everything in the world going for him.

Before black Americans achieved political representation in local and national government, they were represented by black entertainers who shared their background and appreciated their needs. To many, James Brown still articulates their views with greater accuracy and conviction than their more conventional representatives.

Talkin' 'Bout Soul—the Style

Syl Johnson appears at Peacock Alley, a black bar in downtown Minneapolis (Saturday, 23 August 1969). He introduces one of his best known songs, *Different Strokes*, with the words, 'Different strokes for different folks. Special strokes for coloured folks. The reason why we got a special stroke, we coloured folks. That's what makes us soul folks.' People in the closely packed bar chuckle and shout, 'Yeah, tell it Syl', enjoying the subtle innuendo, the circular poetry and the inside references of black dialect. Syl talks to his audience during his version of *Heard It On The Grapevine*, using the roles and the phraseology and imagery of the ghetto as he relates his experiences to those of his listeners. 'You might be a pimp and you might be a hustler. You might be a playboy. But once upon a time there's a woman in your life you really care for. Y'know I live a pretty fast life myself, I know. So I'm gonna get down on my knees and say, "Baby please don't go".' In a lighter vein, Syl produces roars of laughter with a short monologue during *Dresses Too Short*.

> Listen honey. The reason why I don't want you to wear your dresses so short is not because I'm jealous. I ain't *never* jealous. But when you walk down the street I don't want no other man lookin' at your pretty legs. He might see your poo poo. And he might get a notion. He might wanna sock soul power.

The language of soul songs is the dialect of the ghetto. It incorporates many of the hip phrases replete with *double entendre* that typify ghetto parlance. Bill Williams (WCHB) notes the distinctive form of the lyrics of soul music: 'It's definitely a difference in communication because there are certain ways that we say things to each other that we don't say when we're talking to a white person. And it's in soul music too.' Fred Goree

(WCHB) sees the use of ghetto diction and phrasing in soul music as an important aspect of its success,

> This is what it's all about too because it's like easy to relate . . . And it's funny, even those artists who are well educated . . . purposefully revert back to the stereotype form and the bad pronunciation if I can call it that without putting it down, because I think this is where it's really at.

The soul singer thus recognises and relates to his audiences in their own terms, and in doing so at least appears to show them a measure of respect.

As with blues, the music of soul is a language in itself. Raised with the continuity of form of black music, audiences can readily understand and

appreciate this language. Whatever the content of the lyrics, response is geared initially to the form of the music. Butterball (WVON) states,

> Soul music is music that expresses the feeling of the artist, and you find a lot of groups that are singing, you can't even distinguish what they're saying, they're almost unintelligible, but the emotion, the feeling still gets across, the message is across.

The instruments communicate in a similar manner. Butterball continues, 'It can be the music itself, the mood that the music is painting and a guy say, "Ain't that the truth" and "That's what's happenin', baby".' Fred Goree (WCHB) develops this point: 'The guitar and the sax have a way of saying what you can't say orally. They can play it and you can feel it and you say, "Yeah man, I know what you're talkin' about".'

This language of form and style is clearly recognised as a black language. Jack Harris (KUXL) introduces *Until Then I'll Suffer* by Barbara Lynn, 'This is Barbara Lynn. This little lady's got soul, our soul.'

Tell It Like It Is

12th Street, Detroit, a hot, lazy Saturday afternoon in the summer of 1968. A record-shop-cum-shoe-shine parlour, with a speaker mounted over the entrance, blares soul music on to the busy street. The shoe shine boys lounging against the chairs inside break into 'I wanna testify', singing the chorus of Derek Martin's *Soul Power* as it plays to a potential customer. Further down the street four young men in their late teens and early 20s, dressed colourfully in bright purples, oranges and greens, walk along listening to a transistor radio tuned to WCHB, the 'Soul of the City'. The Temptations' oldie *Ain't Too Proud To Beg* is playing and two of them sing along word for word.

Encouraged by singers to 'listen' and 'hear what I say', black audiences listen closely to the words of soul music. A large part of disc-jockey performances is focussed on the lyrics. They anticipate them by quoting a line before its sung and confirm them by repeating or paraphrasing it afterwards. With shouts of 'Go ahead and tell 'em' and 'Talk to me' they emphasise the importance of a song's message. Picking up on vignettes of folk wisdom within a song they summarise the message: 'Yeah, they get the big head when they get some thread on them' is E. Rodney Jones (WVON)'s conclusion to Arthur Connelly's *People Sure Act Funny (When They Get A Little Money)*. Comments on the morality of Clarence Carter's request for the company of another man's wife/girlfriend in *Slip Away* range from 'You just a wrongdoer' from Butterball (WVON) to 'Yeah, it's better when you steals away' from Pervis Spann (WVON).

Like blues, soul music 'tells the truth'. This belief is based on the assumption that the singer has experienced what he is singing about and is expressing what he really feels, and on the fact that the audience can relate to and identify with the music and the story. The belief in the veracity of soul music is seen clearly from the responses of disc-jockeys and of audiences at live performances. 'Alright, there you heard it. He's telling you nothing but the natural truth,' says Ed Cook (WVON) after Joe Tex's *A Woman's Hands*; he then introduces *Think* by Aretha Franklin with the words, 'Here's Aretha, tellin' it like it is.' Stock phrases from the disc-jockey's repertoire include 'You'd better believe it', 'ain't that the truth', 'that's the natural truth', 'tell the truth', 'Yes, yes, yes' and 'tell it like it is', responses echoed by audiences at live performances of soul music.

Like blues, most soul songs tell a story, more often than not of a male-female relationship. 'The songs definitely tell a story, something that people can relate to and identify with', says Jeffrey Troy (WWRL); stories that, in the words of Hal Atkins (WWRL), are 'basically what happens in life'. These stories are seen as realistic reflections of experience. Jerry B. refers to this realism: 'Say like an illegitimate child, yes, it's a natural thing, a part of life, and James Brown or somebody like that wouldn't be afraid to say this to you in his music.'

Both soul music and blues tell a story and tell the truth. Soul music, however, gives a rather different account of the story and a somewhat different version of the truth. These differing perspectives will be illustrated shortly.

It'll Help Your Soul

'Music might not heal you, baby, but it'll help your soul. Reach over and touch your radio one time' says Frankie Crocker, 'The Love Man' (WWRL), over the opening bars of The Temptations' *Please Return Your Love To Me*. Clarence Carter sings *Slip Away* and Joe Cobb (WVON) tells him, 'Go ahead and moan that mess off your chest this afternoon.'

As with blues, a major function of soul music is catharsis. The listener experiences a feeling of emotional relief by hearing his problem related in a song. The recognition, appreciation and understanding a singer shows for a problem makes the situation easier to bear. The listener feels he has someone to share his problem with. Lucky Cordell (WVON) explains a part of the process.

> Hearing it put in a song and seeing that here's a guy who is as bad off as I am, you might even hear the expression, and this might well be where the expression started, 'I know what you mean', because he does know what the singer means because he's living the song.

The expression of individual problems in songs makes them social. They are seen to be shared and appear to be normative. Anxiety is reduced if they are defined as a normal part of life. Joe Cobb (WVON) illustrates this process in action. During Clarence Carter's *Slip Away* Joe Cobb says 'That's alright, son'. He explains,

> It's hard to love another man's wife or girlfriend. Clarence's reasons are all good. We all like have had experience at this and if not we will. I'm saying, That's alright, don't worry, in other words you're not alone, there are millions of others, go ahead.

Defining a problem as normative encourages acceptance of the situation and of human weaknesses and frailties. Songs such as *Everybody Makes a Mistake Sometime* by Mitty Collier and *Temptation Is Hard To Fight* by George McGregor illustrate this perspective. The implication that the problem is rooted in such imponderables as the nature of the situation or human nature encourages philosphical acceptance of what comes. This perspective is less common in soul music than in blues, and as we shall see is balanced by opposite strategies.

The Truth of Soul Music—a Man and a Woman

Soul Music and blues overlap both in the content of their stories and in the attitudes and perspectives they present. However, there are important areas in the one not found or well represented in the other. Beginning with the theme of a man and a woman, we may explore these differences.

The blues singer is largely concerned with unsuccessful relationships. He recounts the breakup of a relationship and expresses the sorrow, and sometimes the bitterness, which results. Rarely does he offer himself as a source of strength to a present or potential partner. In contrast, the soul singer often presents himself as a reliable and dependable partner. In songs such as *You Can Depend On Me* by Luther Ingram and *Lean On Me* by Frederick Knight, comfort and support are promised. In *You Can Depend On Me,* Luther Ingram sings.

> I'll take all of your troubles and cares,
> Just let me know and I'll be right there,
> You got my shoulder to cry on,
> And a trust you can rely on,
> Oh baby, you can depend on me.

A recurring theme in blues is the 'back door man' and his sexual prowess. The emphasis on adultery has largely been replaced in soul music by the lover who offers not only sexual satisfaction, but also comfort and security. In *Soul Man*, Sam and Dave boast about their prowess as lovers but also promise to care for and be faithful to their partners.

> Comin' to you, on a dust road,
> Good lovin', I got a truck load,
> And when you get it, you got somethin',
> So don't you worry, 'cos I'm coming,
> I'm a soul man, I got it all.

> Look! Throw out a rope, and I'll pull you in,
> Give you hope and be your only boy friend.

When the soul singer admits an illicit relationship, he often views it as an unavoidable problem. Rather than condoning it or boasting about it from the amoral stance of the 'back door man', he admits his actions are morally wrong. In *Slip Away* Clarence Carter sings,

> I know it's wrong, the things I ask you to do,
> But please believe me darling, I don't mean to hurt you,
> But could you just slip away, without him knowing you gone,
> Then we could meet somewhere, somewhere where we're both not
>   known.

Whereas the blues singer tends simply to bemoan his fate if his woman is unfaithful, soul singers point to the consequences of illicit relationships and advocate conventional morality. Johnnie Taylor gives the following warning in *Who's Makin' Love,*

> While you're lyin', cheatin' on your woman,
> There is something you never thought of,
> Now tell me who's making love to your old lady,
> While you were out making love.

Johnnie Taylor, who has sung and recorded many blues songs, in the past, compares his theme of today with those of yesterday.

> I'm just tellin' it like it is . . . I could sing songs that in the end condone adultery or playing around with someone's feelings. I have done in the past but that's not where it's at today. So I'm just acknowledging that such situations do exist. But like a preacher I guess I'm tellin' folks that bad will come out of not playing the game right. (*Soul* 17 March 1969: 3)

Whereas blues has little to say about the family, soul songs advocate family stability and parental responsibility. Little Milton begins *If That Ain't A Reason For Your Woman To Leave You* with 'a message for all you so-called men out there', and expresses moral indignation for their erring ways.

> You running round on the corner,
> And you cheatin' too, yes you are,
> Your little kids at home,
> With holes in all their shoes, you ought to be ashamed,
> All the money's in your pocket,
> And the car keys in your hand,
> Instead of takin' care of home,
> You chasin' every woman you can.

In *Believe In Me Baby–Part 2*, Jesse James condemns the opposite sex for similar misdeeds. This record made a tremendous impact when it was first

Left: *Otis Redding*. Right: *Johnnie Taylor*.

heard in Minneapolis on KUXL radio. Listeners swamped the switchboard with requests and it was played five times in the space of two hours.

> But it's only one thing that makes me sick in my heart,
> And that is this. The women out there,
> They won't take care their children.

> When your child wakes up about three o'clock baby,
> And you're not there,
> He begins to get a little worried,
> He needs you home.

On the rare occasions a blues singer mentions his father he is either 'dead and gone', or has turned the singer from his door. The singer's own parental role is noticeable by its absence. Soul songs such as *Color Him Father* by The Winstons and *Let Me Be The Man My Daddy Was* by The Chi-Lites present a picture of the model father and praise his role as a dutiful husband and good provider. The Chi-Lites sing,

> He worked so hard, gentle as a lamb,
> He gave up so much, to make me just what I am.

> And now that I'm a man, I ask the lord up above,
> Please let me raise my children right, and be the man my
>   daddy was.

Work to the blues singer, like life itself, is largely unrewarding. However soul songs sometimes advocate the virtue of work as a factor in family stability and happiness. Presenting their picture of the ideal father, The Winstons begin *Color Him Father* with,

> There's a man at my house, he's so big and strong,
> He goes to work each day and he stays all day long.

In *The Happy Song*, Otis Redding illustrates the rewards of a dutiful and hardworking husband.

> [She] Bring my breakfast to the table,
> When I go to work, she'll know I'm able,
> Do my job, I come back in,
> You oughta see my baby's face,
> She just grin, grin, grin.

Bobby Byrd's advice in *If You Don't Work You Can't Eat* is simple and direct.

> You got to have a job,
> Put meat on the table,
> You got to have a job,
> To keep the family able.

Blues songs tend to state the way things are and offer neither hope nor suggestions for improving the situation. By comparison soul songs advocate the way things should be and are filled with advice for realising this ideal. Songs like *Keep That Man* by Big Maybelle, *Stand By Your man* by Candi Staton and *Keep The One You've Got* By Joe Tex promote the virtues of a stable marriage. Marital stability is stressed not only as a virtue in and of itself, but as a means of mutual support for making it through life. In *Believe In Me Baby—Part 1*, Jesse James is hopeful about the future with his woman's support.

> And though it may seem like we're caught in such a deep
>   deep rut,
> If you only stick with me baby things ought to go way
>   way up,
> We'll make it baby over the bumps.

When a relationship does succeed despite the hardships in its path, the achievement is celebrated. The theme of success through effort, illustrated by Syl Johnson's *We Did It*, is becoming increasingly prominent in soul music.

> It took a whole lots of doing,
> But we did it, yes we did girl,
> It took a lot of doing,
> A lots of renewing,
> We made mistakes,
> But we had what it takes,
> To get over girl.

The simple statement 'My baby left me and I'm sad and lonesome', which forms a dominant theme in blues, is also found in soul music. However, it is often qualified by a plea for the loved one to return and a promise that things will be better. Jimmy 'Soul' Clarke sings in *If Only I Knew Then,*

> If only I knew, what I know about you now,
> Things would've been different.
>
> Give me one more chance, I swear you won't regret it,
> And what you need and what you want, girl you'll get it.

In *Next Time* Johnnie Taylor's situation typifies the blues singer's but his response to it is different.

> When she was here, I cheated and lied,
> Too busy running round, to stop and realise,
> Love is just like a flower, blooms and fades,
> It's here today and tomorrow gone away,
> I'll beg her to take me back, and that is a natural fact,
> This pain and misery, is a little too much for me.
>
> Next time I'll tell her I love her so
>
> So next time I'll do better baby.

Love forms an important theme in soul music. This is partly a reflection of the large black (and indeed white) teenage market catered for. Motown, with its slogan 'The Sound of Young America', puts out scores of teenage-oriented love songs. Some singers, and particularly vocal groups, are supported by a largely teenage audience. A show at Chicago's Regal Theatre (Friday, 12 July 1968) features The Esquires, Bobby Taylor and The Vancouvers, The Jackson Five, Maurice and The Chi-Lites, The Five Artistics, and The Vibrations, vocal groups which emphasise the 'Heaven must have sent you from above' types of lyric. The audience numbers about 700, at least three quarters being children and teenagers. The older people are mainly mothers and relatives who are chaperoning the youngsters. Linda Jones, a more mature singer, is included on the bill for their benefit. However, it would be a mistake to see this emphasis on love as solely a reflection of adolescent tastes. Most singers include songs singing the praises of love in their acts. Singers like Aretha Franklin, Barbara Lynn, Jackie Wilson, Syl Johnson, Johnnie Taylor and James Brown appeal to all age groups. The James Brown show is billed as 'a show for the family' and attracts young and old alike.

Soul music expresses faith in love, hope for love, and the joy and happiness of love. Songs like *I Get The Sweetest Feeling* by Jackie Wilson, *I've Never Found A Girl To Love Me Like You Do* by Eddie Floyd, *What Is This* by Bobby Womack, *You Send Me* by Aretha Franklin and *I Thank*

You by Sam and Dave emphasise the positive rather than the negative side of love. Soul music has its share of sad songs which bemoan lost loves but they do not predominate to the extent found in blues.

In summary, there is an important emphasis in soul music on the way things should be. Whereas blues concentrates almost entirely on experience, usually the experience of failure, soul songs state the ideal. Moral principles are laid down, rules of conduct advocated, right and wrong clearly delineated. Blues has little overt concern with the morality involved. It merely states this is the way it is, and this is how I am suffering. By comparison, soul music implies life is not to be accepted as it comes, hardship is not merely to be borne, but life is to be made worth living. Songs do not gloss over failure or ignore hardship, but point to ways of improving the situation. There is both hope and a remedy for improvement. Lessons are learned from unfortunate experiences which may either patch up existing failure, or give a better chance of success at a future date. The hopes and beliefs articulated are often different from the situation experienced. The image of the future is a good deal better than the present. By comparison blues offers little in the way of hope and optimism; the future, by implication, is a continuation of the present.

Soul music reveals a belief and faith in conventional morality and the protestant ethic as a means to happiness and fulfillment. Role models of the faithful and dutiful husband, the good provider and the responsible father are presented as the ideal. When a relationship succeeds, soul music rejoices in the joy and happiness it brings. Alternative perspectives are found in soul music but the important point is that the perspectives outlined above are either absent from blues or occur with considerably less frequency and conviction.

The Truth of Soul Music–'We're Rolling On'

The Impressions appear at Local 212, Mack, near Connors, Detroit, before a crowd of over 2000, all ages, all black (Saturday, 27 July 1968). Backed by a big band and dressed in well-tailored matching maroon suits, The Impressions open with *Keep on Pushing*, one of their best known songs. People sit drinking at long trestle tables, some sing along, swaying in their seats, sometimes clapping to the rhythm, sometimes holding hands. Younger members of the audience dance at the back of the hall. The atmosphere is festive, smiling faces and party hats. 'Do you feel alright?' asks Curtis Mayfield, The Impressions' lead singer, and the audience shouts its assent; 'Do you feel good?' and the chorus of 'Yeah' is even louder than before. The gospel-based *People Get Ready* follows to shouts of recognition and appreciation and people sing along. A young man turns and says, 'People like their songs because they give them inspiration'. The Impressions sing *We're Rolling On* and dancers link arms, symbolising the message of togetherness in the song. *We're A Winner* is greeted with

The Impressions: Sam Gooden, Curtis Mayfield, Fred Cash.

widespread applause and shouts of 'Yeah', 'Alright' and 'That's right'. The song's message is mirrored on T-shirts worn by several young men and women. Against a black background, 'We're A Winner' is emblazoned across the front in white. The Impressions close their performance with *Amen* and are joined in song by over half the audience.

Reggie Lavong (WWRL) states, 'Soul music is an expression of how we feel today, blues was how we felt yesterday.' The feeling is different and the music is different. Like blues, soul music reflects, defines and directs the strategies, expectations and aspirations of black Americans. However, their content has changed from the days of blues. The strategy of many soul songs is a rejection of the present as undesirable, a refusal to accept the situation, and a determination to create a better future. This strategy is the antithesis of the acceptance of and accommodation to the existing situation which is found in blues. Illustrated by 'We'd rather die on our feet, than keep living on our knees' from James Brown's *Say It Loud*, it is diametrically opposed to, 'I've been down so long that down don't bother me.' In *Freedom Train*, James Carr echoes this refusal to accommodate to the status quo: 'C'mon y'all, we gotta ride the freedom train, we ain't gonna live this way again.' Coupled with this strategy is a moral perspective. The strategy is morally right, the changes it demands are justified. In *Say It Loud*, James Brown sings,

> I say we won't quit moving,
> Until we get what we deserve,
> We've been 'buked and we've been scorned,
> We've been treated bad, as sure as you've been borned,
> But just as it takes two eyes to make a pair,
> We're not gonna quit until we get our share.

Although it offers hope and a promise for the future, soul music still maintains the realism of blues. The hardship and adversity of the present are not ignored. Whereas in blues hardship was a cause for sorrow, sometimes for despair, in soul music it becomes a point of reference for and a spur towards improvement and a better tomorrow. Syl Johnson's *Is It Because I'm Black* describes the situation, points to the cause and advocates the response.

> In this world of no pity,
> I was raised in ghettoes of the city,
> Mama she worked so hard,
> To earn every penny
>
> They're holding us back,
> Y'know why, it is, I believe it's because we're black.
> But hey! We can't stop now, we can't stop now,
> Gotta keep on, keep on, keep on keeping on.

In *Ghetto Man*, Tony Clarke describes a similar background, and asserts his determination to create something better:

> My ma scrubbed floors to keep me clad,
> And me and three brothers had to share one bed,
> When I was young I felt ashamed,
> 'Cos I never knew my papa's name.
> But then out of nowhere I found my pride,
> And I found that a man don't have to hide,
> Some natural love and some good ideas,
> And one of these days you're leaving here,
> With this ghetto man, ghetto man, ghetto man, ghetto man.
>
> C'mon now, up to the top,
> Nobody gonna stop,
> The ghetto man,
> 'Cos he's got a plan.

James Brown uses this antithesis of down and up in his songs and pronouncements. He symbolises the transition from one to the other, his career provides the points of reference. To repeat and continue his statement quoted beforehand, 'This is one cat that knows the meaning of misery. I've been up and I've been down and I know what DOWN is—it's bad. But you can get out of being down, you've got to work and work hard. Like I did, I proved it can be done. So do it!' (*Soul* 3 June 1968: 13).

There is a refusal to accept the world of sorrow portrayed in blues as a definition of the future, and to respond to the present by simply crying about the hardship and sorrow it produces. In *We're A Winner* The Impressions sing,

No more tears do we cry,
And we have finally dried out eyes.
And we're moving on up.

James Brown rejects pity and sympathy in *I Don't Want Nobody To Give Me Nothing*.

Don't give me sorrow,
I want equal opportunity,
To live tomorrow.

We don't want no sympathy.
Just wanna be a man.

Songs such as *People Get Ready, We're A Winner* and *We're Rolling On* by The Impressions, *Free At Last* by James Barnes and The Agents, *Freedom Train* by James Carr and *Freedom Means* by The Dells present a picture and a vision of the future. It is a future which is on hand and drawing nearer. These songs, which often employ imagery found in gospel music, are full of hope and enthusiasm, movement and anticipation. In *We're Rolling On* The Impressions sing,

People get ready,
I got good news for you,
How we got over,
Like we all supposed to do.
Let us all say amen,
And together we'll clap our hands,
'Cos we're rolling on
Lord it's hard times,
And it's hard climb,
But we cannot stop until we reach that mountain top.

The emphasis is not on the individual but on the whole group moving forward together, and working for the future together. In *Freedom Train* James Carr uses the train imagery so often found in gospel music, only this time the train is not going to heaven.

Your freedom train is coming,
Can't you hear the whistle blowing,
It's time to get your tickets y'all,
And get on board.
It's time for all the people,
To take the freedom ride,
Now take it together,
And work for freedom side by side.

Backed by a gospel piano and gospel harmonies, The Dells in *Freedom Means* define what the future should be and encourage their audience to translate it into reality.

> Freedom means being able to say what's on your mind,
> And speak right out and talk about the things we know that
>   should be better,
> And freedom means being able to make your space in time,
> And if we try there's no doubt we can work it all out together,
> Sister lend a helping hand, and brother heed the call,
> A brand new day is dawning on us all.

The traditional American ideals of hard work and a good education are part of the means for realising this future. James Brown's million seller *Don't Be A Dropout*, with its chorus 'Without an education, might as well be dead', tells the story of a high school dropout who compares himself with his successful friends who 'follow the rules'.

> So one day he got tired of his little spending change,
> So he looked up his friends, and checked their pay rate,
> When he got there he found he was a drag,
> 'Cos man they were clean and his clothes were like rags.
> One was a businessman with plenty of dough,
> Had his thing so set up, you know he couldn't blow,
> The other had his job so uptight,
> He had his whole family and his kids all out of sight.
> For his friends they worked real hard, when they worked their
>   way through,
> Now he realised he should have done the same thing too.
>
> They kept on pushin' when the going was tough,
> And now they know that things don't seem so rough,
> So kids, stay in school. Don't be no drag.

In *Color Him Father* The Winstons place a similar emphasis upon education and advocate a policy of following 'the golden rule'.

Soul music promotes black self-help and mutual aid as a further means for realising the future. In several songs James Brown argues the case for black unity and for blacks working together for their mutual benefit. In *I Don't Want Nobody To Give Me Nothing* he sings,

> We got talents we can use,
> For our side of town,
> Let's get ahead together,
> And build it up from the ground,
> When some of us make money,
> We must care about our people.

Concern is expressed in soul music for conditions in the poorer areas of black society. In blues, these conditions are seen, by implication, as imponderables within which the individual must somehow survive. In soul music they are condemned and defined as something to be eradicated. The use of drugs forms the subject of a number of blues and soul songs. The blues singer puts himself in the position of the drug addict, sings about the experience, and either bemoans his fate seeing no way out of the situation, or describes, with some bravado, the pleasure he obtains. Soul singers are concerned with creating a climate and a frame of mind which can do something about the problem. Drug abuse is condemned by the Dramatics in *The Devil Is Dope* and James Brown in *King Heroin* and *Public Enemy No.1*. In one of the first soul songs advocating positive action against drug abuse, *(We Gotta) Bust Out Of The Ghetto*, recorded in 1970, Moody Scott sings,

> You know it's sad, it's so sad,
> The young man is throwing his life away.
> Now people out there you know it's not right,
> 'Cos it's not supposed to be that way.
> We got to stop the pusher man,
> Messing with our children.

Former Vice-President Hubert Humphrey congratulates James Brown on the success of Don't Be A Dropout.

Associated with the new hopes and strategies presented in soul music are new definitions and evaluations of blackness. Strategies focussing upon improvement and positive definitions of blackness are often contained and related within the same song. In *Say It Loud* James Brown sings,

> But we'd rather die on our feet,
> Than keep living on our knees,
> Say it loud, I'm black and I'm proud

Jerry B. responds to these sentiments as he introduces *Say It Loud* on WWRL, New York.

> Hey baby, if you're like me you've watched that television commercial on which the young man states that it's true that blondes have more fun. And I got brainwashed myself and I wanted to find out if it was true that blondes had more fun. So I dyed my hair and now I ain't got none. So I reorganised my philosophy and my way of thinking and now I've reached the conclusion that if I have but one life to live, let me live it with my afro. I'm black and I'm proud and I am what I am y'all.

The white definition of blackness, so often reflected in blues with lines like 'Black man is evil' from *Chocolate To The Bone* by Barbecue Bob, has been replaced by an affirmation of blackness as worthwhile. *Say It Loud* is probably the most effective vehicle to counter the 'brainwashing' referred to by B.B. King in Chapter 2 and by Jerry B. above. Replete with the hip catchphrases of ghetto dialect, it states,

> Say it loud, I'm black and I'm proud
> Whee it's hurting me, if it's alright, it's alright,
> You're too tough, you're tough enough,
> You're alright and you're out of sight,
> Say it loud, I'm black and I'm proud.

Shortly after this record was released James Brown stopped processing his hair and grew an afro, explaining '. . . we need an identity. Our people need to know who they are and I think a natural helps remind us of ourselves' (*Soul* 17 March 1969: 17). This perspective is reflected in *I Don't Want Nobody To Give Me Nothing* in which James demands

> Give me schools, and give me better books,
> So I can read about myself, and gian my true looks.

Soul songs relate blackness to beauty—*Black Pearl* by Sonny Charles—and ability—*Young, Gifted and Black* by Nina Simone—and determination to make it—*We're A Winner* by The Impressions. Curtis Mayfield, the leader of The Impressions (he has since taken up a solo career), explains his approach.

> Our purpose is to educate as well as to entertain. Painless preaching is as good a term as any for what we do. If you're going to come

away from a party singing the lyrics of a song, it is better that you sing of self-pride like *We're A Winner* instead of *Do The Boo-ga-loo!* (*Soul* 22 September 1969: 16)

Throughout these songs there is an emphasis upon togetherness in general and black unity in particular. The definition of blackness they contain denies the divisions within black society based on degrees of blackness, a status hierarchy that forms the theme of many blues. Syl Johnson sings in *Is It Because I'm Black*, 'Y'see if you have white light brown skin and a high yellow, you're still black, so we got to stick together now.' Reflecting this togetherness the 'I' of blues is often replaced by the 'we' of soul music. Butterball (WVON) comments upon this change,

The old blues singer's sayin' no matter what the world is makin' out of you, how you allowing the world to twist your mind and break your spirits down, I'm gonna keep on pushin', I'm gonna get by somehow. A blues singer always sings about himself most of the time. The new breed now, or the soulful people instead of the blues people, which are still soulful, but I'm saying the new breed, they're talkin' about this togetherness because it's more united now. Years ago they were individuals and they had individualistic attitudes. Now they say we're rolling on, we're gonna keep on pushin', we're gonna make it. It's the togetherness. I guess its a movement.

This unity is reflected in live performances of soul music. At a blues show, listeners respond as individuals. But when James Brown invites members of his audience to sing a response, they answer in unison. When the Impressions sing *We're A Winner* people link arms and join in on the chorus.

Songs such as *We're A Winner* and *Say It Loud* referring directly and explicitly to black pride and self-determination first began to appear in 1968. However, the perspectives and strategies they promote were present in soul music before that date. Though the vehicle is different the attitudes reflected in the songs analysed under the headings of 'A Man And A Woman' and 'We're Rolling On' are similar. Songs have tended to move from depicting individual relationships from which a general message can be drawn, to an explicit proclamation of that message. In 1965 Otis Redding recorded *Respect*, in which he asked his wife for a little respect when he got home. In 1967 Aretha Franklin recorded the same song with a change of gender. By 1970 in *To The Other Man,* Luther Ingram was advocating respect for others as a general guide for living. In 1971 the Staple Singers in *Respect Yourself* announced to everybody, 'It's a brand new day. Respect yourself.' Johnnie Taylor's songs show this move from the particular to the general. In *Mr Nobody Is Somebody*, recorded in 1969, he compares himself with his successful friends who regard him as a failure. He maintains that he is 'somebody' because he has found happiness and fulfilment in love. However, in *I Am Somebody*, recorded in 1970, he moves beyond the personal and particular, includes his audience directly in the song, and proclaims unconditionally, 'I am somebody, you are somebody.'

It is difficult to measure the effect of the messages contained within soul music since they both reflect and direct. In general we may point to the fact that most black Americans hear the more popular soul records. They can relate to and identify with the music. The language is that of the ghetto and the singer a man of the people. Mavis Staples gives her views of the results of the Staple Singers' music: 'I truly think it helps unity and that's one of the things we are striving for . . . A lot of young people have told us that they go away from our shows with the single aim of trying to do better by people.' (*Blues and Soul* 90: 8). We may make a few suggestive observations about *Say It Loud* and *We're A Winner*. Both songs reached Number 1 in most charts compiled by black radio stations, and were played regularly on those stations. At a conservative estimate well over half the black radio audience heard them. Many thousands heard them at live performances. In black theatres across the United States James Brown sang *Say It Loud* and entire audiences shouted back 'I'm black and I'm proud'. Waiting to buy their tickets for The Impressions, parts of the crowd sang *We're A Winner* while vendors did brisk business with 'We're A Winner' T-shirts. Black students at Howard University, Washington D.C., having won their demands for a black research institute, celebrated their success by singing *We're A Winner*. The titles of and quotations from these songs are written on walls in ghetto areas. Store windows are boarded up after the disturbances of 1968 on Selby Avenue, the main route through the black ghetto of St Paul, Minnesota. At the corner of Selby and Fisk, on brown plywood in black spray-paint is written 'Say it loud, I'm black and I'm proud'. One block down at Selby and Victoria, 'I'd rather die on my feet than keep living on my knees' is sprayed crudely across the store front. At a minimum these songs reflect and symbolise the attitude of many black Americans. To go a step further they probably reinforce these attitudes, and to go even further they may even, for some, initiate them. Job Cobb (WVON) gives his view:

> *We're Rolling On* and songs like that gave a lot of people, and even a lot of civil rights organisations, hope and great strength, and made people believe into it, because actually within the record itself, it was telling you like what to expect, and what had happened thus far, so like hold your head up high and keep on going, your day will come.

Soul music probably reaches a larger black public than any other medium. It makes normative the messages it contains.

Over page: *the late King Curtis.*

Soul Music and Soul

Jerry B. talks about soul over the closing bars of *Listen Here* by Eddie Harris, on WWRL New York.

> Radio got soul, I got soul, our newsman got soul, everybody got soul on the big RL. Soul is being able to have fun and not necessarily be a blonde. Are you with that? Soul is being able to do what you wanna do, when you can do it, because you wanna do it, while you can do it. Do it to it. Soul is being able to raise cornbread in your back yard and not be troubled by the city farming ordinance. That's what soul is baby. Soul is Eddie Harris playin' *Listen Here*.

Soul songs define and articulate the concept of soul and the music itself forms a part of that concept. James Brown is known as 'Soul Brother Number One' and Aretha Franklin as 'Soul Sister Number One'. To further understand and appreciate the importance of soul music in black America, it is necessary to see it in relation to soul.

The terms 'soul brother', 'soul sister' and 'soul people' have had increasing currency in black society throughout the '60s. They have various connotations. They are alternative terms of reference for black. During the ghetto riots of the '60s, store owners painted 'soul' and 'soul brother' on their premises to identify them as black-owned, hoping thus to save them from looting and damage. A soul brother is 'someone who is one of the group', membership being a de facto status because 'we're all in the same pot'. Members have experienced a similar initiation into the group; to qualify for membership they have 'paid their dues' by 'coming up the hard way', that is, by growing up black in America. Soul brothers share common understandings which have resulted from these shared experiences. A soul brother is 'someone you can feel real communication with, someone who understands; we've all been through it so we know what it's all about.' Associated with the insets played on black radio in which James Brown exhorts 'This is James Brown—be a soul brother' is the idea that 'Soul brothers have a sense of understanding about themselves to a point where they're not confused. They have some type of direction, something going for them. They are together' (Jeffrey Troy, WWRL). As Soul Brother Number One James Brown epitomises the status and the role.

'Soul' is also applied to food. In *Soul Food* Johnny Watson sings the praises of the traditional black diet with lines like 'Girl if you want a friend right till the end, just put some neckbones on my plate.' Though soul food was also eaten by poor Southern whites, in general only blacks have continued its use in the North, where it is exclusively associated with them. The soul food menu includes the cheaper cuts from the pig, neckbone, hamhocks, pig's ears, hog jowls, fatback pork, chitlins, and collard and turnip greens, black-eyed peas, grits (a kind of porridge) and corn bread. The essence of soul food according to many blacks is that it is 'basic', and its cooking techniques preserve the 'goodness' of the food. According to one soul food connoisseur,

> The white man used to take the steak and give the black man the gravy, and when he would boil some greens, he'd give the black man the pot liquor to soak his cornbread in. It took him a hundred years to figure out he was giving the Negro all the nutrients and all he was getting was the waste. (*Newsweek* 18 September 1967: 100)

Soul food restaurants are found in the black ghettoes of the North but they are far outnumbered by the more conventional American eating establishments such as McDonald's Hamburgers. In the urban environments of the North soul food occurs more frequently in conversations than on the table. Eaten formerly because of economic necessity, it has been raised to the status of a delicacy, and its importance is as much symbolic as gastronomic.

Soul songs occasionally wax lyrical about soul food, and soul food is used metaphorically to refer to soul music. The configuration is neatly tied up in *Memphis Soul Stew* by tenor saxophonist King Curtis. The spoken introduction outlines the recipe and brings in the various instruments, the ingredients of the music.

> Today's special is Memphis Soul Stew,
> We sell so much of this, people wonder what we put in it,
> We gonna tell you right now.
> Give me about half a teacup of bass,
> Now I need a pound of fat back drums,
> Now give me four tablespoons of bawlin' Memphis guitar,
> This is gonna taste alright.
> Now just a little pinch of organ,
> Now give me half a pint of horn,
> Place it on the burner and bring to the boil,
> That's it! That's it! That's it right there!
> Now beat, well!

Disc-jockeys respond to soul music with exclamations of 'cook!' and 'burn!' and comments like 'That sounds like cornbread and beans.' The phrase 'Ain't that the nitty gritty', possibly deriving from grits, is often used to describe a soul record. Ed Cook (WVON) explains nitty gritty and interrelates soul food and soul music: 'Soul music gets down to the bare facts of the truth; that's what nitty gritty means. In other words it's like eating soul food, white beans, grits and gravy, corn pone or what have you, the bare essentials.' Clearly a similarity of essence is perceived in soul people, soul music and soul food. In Fred Goree's (WCHB) words, 'There's a sameness about them all.' Soul recognises this sameness and acts as a unifying symbol.

Soul denotes approbation, it is a term of approval. As a quality of self it is highly valued. To suggest one has no soul or has lost his soul, is, in the words of one informant, 'the most hurting thing for a Negro.' The value of soul is referred to in many soul songs. *It's Alright* by The Impressions has the chorus

> If you got soul,
> Everybody knows,
> That it's alright.

In *Soul People* Shan Miles proclaims,

> Worth more than gold,
> You can't buy soul.

As a personal attribute, 'you get soul by coming up the hard way, by paying your dues.' Soul 'develops from hurt and pain; you have to have been through it to have it.' Soul is viewed both as a product of black experience and as a necessary condition for black survival. Lucky Cordell (WVON) states, 'If you have soul you can make it. It's like saying if you hang on in there, if you hang on in there, if you have what it takes, you can make it if you have soul.' Many soul songs refer to the ability and determination to make it and some explicitly relate this to soul. In *Keep On Pushing* The Impressions sing, 'I know I can make it with just a little bit of soul.'

A further use of the term 'soul' is to refer to aspects of behaviour seen as characteristic of an approved black style. A song by Dyke and The Blazers entitled *We Got More Soul* illustrates this usage.

> Tellin' the world,
> Sisters and my brothers,
> We got more soul,
> When we walk,
> We got more soul, we got it,
> When we talk,
> We got more soul, we got it,
> When we sing, Lord have mercy,
> We got more soul, we got it,
> When we dance,
> We got more soul.

Discussing soul, informants often refer to the manner in which blacks walk, talk, sing and dance as indicative of soul. Typical statements are, 'A Negro, he walks a little different, he talks a little different and there's a tightness in this thing', and 'We don't cut no corners as far as, like, "my baby ain't gonna cook no beans tonight", the way it's phrased, the way it's said, this is considered soul.' The standard of comparison for this black style is a white American middle-class style. Butterball Jr. (WCHB) states, 'This midwest deal [standard American English] . . . we were trained in this here talk by the white man, and it's correct pronunciation whenever you're in a position to use it. But not when you're into a bag like you are with the fellas.' Implicit in many statements is that a black style of behaviour is the expression of the real self: 'When you get down

DYKE
AND THE
BLAZERS

DYKE'S GREATEST HITS LP#8877

with the people you have to be in your bag. Like for instance we'd be saying, "Say man, dig" or "brother, what's happenin', it's your world, I'm just living in it." This is the natural being. Soul is being yourself.'

Soul symbolises the re-evaluation and re-definition of black identity, experience, behaviour and culture. Soul associates those aspects considered essentially black and stamps them with a seal of approval. Black is no longer inferior, no longer a poor copy of white. It is distinct and different and glossed with the term 'soul' is worth having and worth being.

The connotations of soul clearly dovetail with the meanings and associations black people see in soul music. Soul singers are seen to express soul in their performances. Their music exemplifies a black style and their songs portray the black experience. Fred Goree (WCHB) explains the symbolic importance of soul music.

> Calling it soul music is a way of identifying it, putting a stamp on it, and saying soul music is ours. Every nationality has to make its own way, but none have had to travel the route the black man has had to

travel. That's where we got soul and there's a lot of racial pride wrapped up in this. The black man personifies the black race singing with soul. The black man knows where it's at when it comes to singing with soul because he's been through it and when he sings it's exemplified in him.

Jeffrey Troy (WWRL) explains why soul music is a central feature of the concept of soul.

Soul music maintains a hell of a lot of importance because it is one of the very few things in this country that the black man can say is his. It's a part of his identification and very important for image making purposes.

When James Brown as Soul Brother Number One says something, his words are backed by the system of meanings and associations that make up the concept of soul. When Brown recorded *Don't Be A Dropout*, it sold a million. However, when the Stax Recording Company attempted to follow his lead it was less successful. Large red plastic letters spelt out SOULSVILLE U.S.A. on the facade of the old movie theatre Stax had converted into a recording studio in Memphis. The letters were changed to STAY IN SCHOOL and were promptly stoned by youngsters in the neighbourhood until the original message was restored.

Gospel and Soul Music

We now return to the question of the synthesis of musical styles that became soul music, and in particular ask why gospel music was incorporated to become the most important element from the past.

Any change is never a complete change, it is based on developments and syntheses of past models. The first, though not the primary, reason for the selection of gospel music is its availability. As an important musical tradition, it was understood and appreciated and could serve its new purpose without a radical musical re-training of those who were to sing soul music.

A second and more important reason for the incorporation of gospel music is the perspective it contains. In the words of one of the Ward Sisters, (a gospel group), 'For people who work hard and make little money, it offers a promise that things will be better in the life to come' (Frazier 1966: 74). According to Thomas A. Dorsey, one of the founders of modern gospel music, 'Make it anything than good news and it ceases to be gospel' (Heilbut 1971: 70). Many gospel songs ring with jubilation and triumph, conviction and anticipation about reaching the 'blessed home-land,' 'moving on up a little higher' and 'waking up in glory.' The themes are structured on the same basic equation, the opposition of present and future, of pain and joy. The hardships of the present on earth are catalogued and compared with the happiness of the future in heaven. Even

Above: *Chapel of Hope, Chicago—the message of hope that preceded soul.*
Right: *Bobby Bland.*

the most mournful gospel songs are not intrinsically despondent, since they offer ultimate salvation. With the qualification that the life to come is on earth and not in heaven, the perspective of gospel music fits the mood of black Americans in the '60s. The agency responsible for the life to come is secular, not sacred. In the same way gospel music has become secular as soul music. The future orientation, the hope and the promise of gospel music all fit the expressive needs of the '60s and '70s.

A third reason for the transformation of gospel music into soul is its ethical stance. Gospel music advocates a moral position and states the way things ought to be. It does this in two ways. Firstly, by presenting a picture of heaven and by implication the way things ought to be on earth.

Heaven is a place of love and beauty where mutual respect, freedom and justice are found. Secondly, gospel music is concerned with the Christian morality and the Christian ideal, of living the gospel life on earth, both for its own sake and as a means of salvation. The message for earth is the strictures of the Ten Commandments rather than the politics of Black Power. Again gospel music largely equates with the secular perspectives of the era. Soul music advocates conventional morality in terms of individual relationships, states the ideal for the broader framework of society and presents a picture of the way life ought to be. This realtionship between soul and gospel music is seen from Bobby Bland's comments about the songs he has recorded. His favourites are those closest to gospel music,

> My favourite is *I'll Take Care of You* and *Lead Me On*, because they're more of a spiritual touch to it. Because, y'see, I picture a lot of things, y'know, how things really should be, and some notes that I sing on stage, I have to close my eyes because I can visualise, y'know, the word and the thought, and I put them together and it makes a beautiful picture.

Curtis Mayfield (left) *and The Impressions.*

The Impressions' songs are strongly gospel-influenced. Their former leader and songwriter, Curtis Mayfield, explains why he uses this vehicle to make his point. 'For message songs I believe in gospel music very strongly, simply because gospel tunes do carry a greater message and they're usually very inspiring' (*Soul* 22 September 1969: 17). Bill Williams (WCHB) notes the needs of the black audience:

> I have found as music director that the audience looks for more of a message in soul tunes than they look for in other kinds of music. And this is where we get the gospel thing, the roots of soul music, for gospel songs always carried a message of some sort.

The most important message is summarised by Hal Atkins (WWRL): 'The hope of a new day is in everything now and that's why you get gospel in soul music.'

Finally, the theme of togetherness in soul music is reflected in both the themes and the structure of gospel music. In time members of the congregation would share the promised land and live together in harmony. This is reflected in the communal structure of gospel music, in its call and response pattern and its vocal harmonies. These aspects have continued in soul music, symbolising the increasing unity of soul people.

In terms of both its perspective and its musical structure, gospel music was pre-adapted to the secular needs of black musical expression.

4/Soul People

In *Time Has Brought About A Change*, a quiet reflective song, Willie Hightower summarises an era. He sings about the results of change that most songs only anticipate. Though he describes and affirms his experience in personal terms, the message remains sufficiently general for members of his audience to relate to it both their particular experience and the overall course of events.

> That old life that I onced lived,
> Oh I could never live it again,
> And the treatment that I once received,
> They could never be accepted anymore,
> The mistakes that I once made,
> Oh, I won't ever make them again,
> Because I know, oh yes I know,
> That time, oh time, has brought 'bout a change.
>
> Once I, I was a considerate man,
> Given no respect at all,
> But oh now I've got my pride,
> Deep down inside,
> And no one will ever take it again.
>
> That old life that I once lived
> Oh I would never, I would never, no, no, no,
> Live it again,
> Because I know,
> I know that you know that I know,
> That time, oh time, has brought 'bout a change.
> Oh yes it has.

In this chapter we examine the changes in black American society that are related to changes in black music, and outline the events that are anticipated by Sam Cooke's *A Change Is Gonna Come* and confirmed by Willie Hightower's *Time Has Brought About A Change.*

The Decline of Jim Crow

Prior to 1954 Jim Crow was a legal and social reality. The majority of black Americans either acted in terms of its proscriptions or escaped to urban ghettoes where they had at least an illusion of freedom. Following World War II, the first organised protest against the Jim Crow system was conducted by the NAACP (National Association for the Advancement of

Colored People). This organisation was composed largely of middle- and upper-class blacks and white middle-class liberals. The NAACP was not actively supported by the black masses, it did not catch their imagination or afford them much hope. It focussed its attack upon segregation and operated mainly through legal channels, appealing ultimately to the public and judicial conscience of white America. In 1954, a case brought by the NAACP concerning segregation in schools reached the Supreme Court. This led to the famous 'Brown decision' which declared the so-called 'separate but equal' principle in education to be unconstitutional, and so provided the first major piece of civil rights legislation of the century. This decision marked the beginning of the end for Jim Crow. However, there was no immediate outburst of protest against the system, though the following year it appears that the initiative of the NAACP and the Supreme Court was beginning to make an impression. In 1955 the NAACP filed petitions against segregation in schools, signed by local blacks, with 170 school boards in 17 states (Vann Woodward 1966: 154).

December 1955 marked a change in strategy, with the onset of direct action by local blacks against the Jim Crow system. In Montgomery, Alabama, Mrs Rosa Parks, a black lady, refused to give up her seat on a bus to a white man. This began the Montgomery bus boycott involving thousands of blacks, many of whom walked to work for over six months. Litigation brought by the NAACP resulted in the Federal District Court ordering in 1956, that segregation on buses in Montgomery must end. This was the first time that a movement, initiated by and composed of large numbers of locally based black people, had successfully attacked Jim Crow. It began an end to the posture of submission and passivity that blacks had been forced to maintain. Dr Martin Luther King, who had risen to prominence with the Montgomery boycott, formed the Southern Christian Leadership Council to coordinate and organise local efforts against segregation across the South.

Times were changing, but changing slowly. In 1961, seven years after the Brown decision, the percentage of blacks in public schools with whites in 11 Southern states ranged from 0% in three States up to 1.4% in one state (Franklin and Starr 1967: 303). In 1960, Jim Crow was more or less intact, blacks were still denied the vote in large areas of the South, and discrimination and segregation were largely unchanged.

What had been scattered and largely discontinuous attacks against Jim Crow changed in 1960, a year that has been termed 'the year of massive awakening' for black America (Vann Woodward 1965: 169). In 1960, four young black college students in Greensboro, North Carolina, sat down at the all-white lunch counter at Woolworth's and asked politely to be served. When they were refused, they continued to 'sit in'. This prom ted direct action on a massive scale and students, with varying degrees of success,

Left: *Willie Hightower, Apollo Theatre, New York.*

attacked segregation in public places across the South. Figures show the rising tide of protest. In 1961 more than 50,000 people, mostly black, were involved in civil rights demonstrations. By 1963, there were over 2000 demonstrations, with hundreds of thousands participating (Segal 1967: 254).

In 1960, shortly after the Greensboro sit-in, the Student Non-Violent Co-ordinating Committee (SNCC) was formed. It represented an important break with the past. The NAACP was composed mainly of middle-aged blacks working through legislative channels, with white support. SNCC was made up largely of young blacks who put their faith in direct action. The NAACP and the courts had lost the initiative. Black people were in charge of their own movement, which, according to Vann Woodward, represented as much an uprising of youth against parental Uncle Toms, as a black revolt against whites (Vann Woodward 1966: 170).

Black protest was dramatised in 1963, by the march on Washington of nearly a quarter of a million people. About 20% of the marchers were white, and 'black and white together' was a recurrent chant, an emphasis that, in a few years, was to change. The demands of the marchers saw the beginning of new perspectives. Economics issues assumed greater importance and the need for jobs was stressed. The marchers sang spirituals and gospel songs en route, and Mahalia Jackson shared the podium in Washington with Martin Luther King. Gospel music was now relating to the politics of earth as well as those of heaven. Dr King delivered his famous 'I have a dream' speech, and the phrase captured the mood of many black Americans. It became the slogan for WCHB radio in Detroit, and is used on the thousands of bumper stickers that station distributes. The Federal Government responded to black protest in general, and the Washington march in particular, with the 1964 Civil Rights Act, which aimed at ending discrimination based on race in employment, voting, justice and education. Events showed the difficulty of translating parts of this Act into reality. In Mississippi and Selma, Alabama, attempts by blacks to register to vote met with strong and often violent white resistance. This led to the 1965 Voting Rights Act, a more comprehensive and effective law. As a legal entity, Jim Crow was now dead.

The period 1954 to 1965 had begun with a small white liberal and black middle-class organisation, the NAACP, attacking Jim Crow by propoganda and legal action, with little interest or support from the masses of black Americans. The period ended with a movement led by and largely composed of black people, using a strategy of direct non-violent action against segregation. Large numbers of traditionally submissive Southern blacks successfully demonstrated against the system which had contained them for over half a century.

Throughout these years gospel music was increasingly heard in secular contexts. Demonstrators took gospel songs out of the churches and on to the streets. At the sit-ins and marches against segregation in Birmingham,

Black leaders meet newsmen outside the White House, following their meeting with President Kennedy to discuss the racial crisis in Birmingham, Ala., September 1963. The Rev. Martin Luther King stands at the microphones; on his right is the Rev. Ralph D. Abernathy.

Alabama, in 1963, crowds chanted 'Freedom' in unison with gospel fervour and sang the traditional gospel song recorded as *Amen* by The Impressions. In the same year The Impressions recorded the gospel-based *People Get Ready* which became a best-seller, reflecting the spirit of anticipation and momentum. Gospel songs were adapted to meet the new situation. *We'll Never Turn Back* was the theme song for the Mississippi Summer Project, a campaign to register black voters in 1964. It translated a traditional gospel theme into a freedom song.

> We've been 'buked and we've been scorned,
> We've been turned back sure's you're born,
> But we'll never turn back,
> No, we'll never turn back,
> Till all people be free,
> And we have equality.

(Garland 1969: 40-1).

Events imbued soul songs, such as Little Milton's *We're Gonna Make It*, recorded in 1965, with a new significance. Gospel singers began to direct their music to the changing times. In March 1965, Dr King organised a march from Selma, Alabama, to the state capital, Montgomery, to demonstrate against discrimination in voter registration. This event prompted the Staple Singers to begin their move from gospel to soul, and to direct their music to the future on earth. They recorded an album entitled *Freedom Highway* to commemorate the march. Their leader, Roebuck Staples, says of the album,

The Staple Singers.

> We recorded that one in a church. It was just after the march from
> Selma to Montgomery, down in Alabama. Lot of people got hurt
> then, lot of people. I'm for the freedom movement, that's why it
> was recorded. It's about Highway 80. That one goes through Selma
> and Montgomery. We've traveled that road many times, played all up
> and down there. The album is dedicated to all the freedom marchers.
> (*R 'n' B World* 17 October 1968: 6)

With the advantage of hindsight, Mavis Staples sees the importance of the
Selma march on the course of the Staple Singers' music. She also
recognizes the closeness of gospel and soul music. In 1972, when the
transition to soul music is complete, she says,

> Our material hasn't changed a great deal over the years. Maybe we've
> switched from mostly gospel to mostly message songs. That was a
> move which began some years ago when daddy wrote a song to
> commemorate Dr King's march from Montgomery to Selma. He
> called it *Freedom Highway*, and it's been his inspiration since. (*Blues
> & Soul* 90: 8)

The Rise of Black Power

Black protest in the South was accompanied by demonstrations in Northern and West Coast cities. The movement was national and received considerable publicity at all levels. Presidents Kennedy and Johnson frequently broadcast their commitment to civil rights, on radio and T.V. President Johnson promised to deal not only with the institution of Jim Crow but also with its consequences. With regard to the employment, health, housing and welfare of black Americans he pledged, 'To all these fronts—and a dozen more—I will dedicate the expanding efforts of the Johnson administration' (Franklin and Starr 1967: 230). Blacks had been guaranteed equality of opportunity under the law and promised assistance to realise it. Their expectations for improvement increased to a point which several commentators describe as a 'revolution in rising expectations.'

Particularly in Northern and West Coast inner city ghettoes, these expectations did not harmonise with reality. In the face of de facto segregation, chronic unemployment, poverty and urban decay, any advances fell far short of what many felt justified in expecting. Frustration in the big city ghettoes grew as the gap between expectations and reality widened. Against this background the riots of the '60s exploded. Beginning with Harlem in 1964, followed by Watts in 1965 and culminating in Detroit and Newark in 1967, the focus of black protest turned to social and economic deprivation rather than the more obvious manifestations of Jim Crow. The US Riot Commission summarises the motives of rioters: 'What the rioters appeared to be seeking was fuller participation in the social order and the material benefits enjoyed by the majority of American citizens' (National Advisory Commission 1968: 7). The most widely and intensely held grievances of the rioters were listed by the Commission as police practices, unemployment and under-employment, sub-standard housing, inadequate education, poor recreation facilities and programmes, and the ineffectiveness of the political structure and grievance mechanisms (National Advisory Commission 1968: 6-7). As a response to this situation the 'Black Power Movement' emerged.

Beginning as a slogan and a programme for the future, black power reflected and crystallised the mood of many black Americans. Outlined by two of its early spokesmen, Stokely Carmichael and Charles V. Hamilton,

> It is a call for black people in this country to unite, to recognise their heritage, to build a sense of community. It is a call for black people to begin to define their own goals, to lead their own organisations and support those organisations . . . The concept of Black Power rests on a fundamental premise: Before a group can enter the open society, it must first close ranks. By this we mean that group solidarity is necessary before a group can operate effectively from a bargaining position of strength in a pluralistic society. (Carmichael and Hamilton 1969: 58).

The emphasis upon breaking down the barriers of Jim Crow was shifted to a determination to build up the power of the black community. Whereas Martin Luther King had hoped to bring change by demonstrating to white Americans 'our capacity to suffer', Stokely Charmichael advocated black economic and political power as a prerequisite to and a means for entering into the mainstream of society. As a strategy, black power reduced still further the role of whites and placed black destiny more in black hands.

From the mid-'60s there was a growing realisation that constitutional guarantees were insufficient to guarantee blacks an equal place in American society. Jim Crow might be legally dead but its legacy remained. The initial response to this realisation, the rhetoric of black power, was slowly translated into action. The career of Jesse L. Jackson illustrates this process. As one of Dr King's deputies, Jesse Jackson participated in the crusades of the early '60s, before turning directly to the problems of the urban ghettoes. Beginning in Chicago in 1966, Jackson organised 'Operation Breadbasket' to boycott ghetto supermarkets which employed few blacks on their staff. By 1970 he had created over 5,000 new jobs for ghetto residents. Jackson used the power of his organisation to demand that stores in black areas deposit their takings in ghetto banks, thus maintaining capital within the community. To support incipient black capitalism, he demanded that stores prominently display the products of black companies, such as Mumbo barbecue sauce, Joe Louis milk and King Solomon spray deodorant (*Time* 6 April 1970: 12). Jackson's philosophy echoes Carmichael's programme;

> We're already separate and blacks didn't do the separating—and we don't have the power to do the integrating. So the question becomes whether we remain separate and dependent, or become separate and independent—obviously that's the way we've got to go. (Ibid. 12)

Jackson has set up 'Operation Breadbasket' in eight major cities, and in Cleveland the organisation became involved in the election of the city's first black mayor, Carl Stokes. It sent its band on a tour of the ghetto at five o'clock in the morning and irate and bewildered residents were told to get up and vote early for Stokes. James Brown's message *Get Up, Get Into It, Get Involved,* the title of one of his hit records, was seen in action. Jesse Jackson himself advocates and gives his personal support to black political power. In 1970, he was a prominent speaker at the election of Newark's first black mayor, Kenneth Gibson, proclaiming, 'We are the new people . . . When Martin Luther King crossed the mountaintop, I believe he saw Newark on the other side', while in the streets exhuberant blacks danced and shouted, 'Right on! Right on!', 'Things gonna be all right', and 'Ain't we so beautiful' (*Newsweek* 29 July 1970: 26). The Hallelujah days of the early '60s when Dr King had appeared with gospel and spiritual singers were replaced by soul singers James Brown and Stevie Wonder performing as a part of Mayor Gibson's electoral campaign.

The slogan of the Black Panthers, reflected in song by The Chi-Lites' record of *Power to the People* is slowly becoming a reality. Black Americans now see their political potential as an important means for improving their situation. By 1970 black mayors were installed in Cleveland, Newark, Washington, D.C., Gary, Indiana, and in the small town of Fayette, Mississippi. An opinion poll conducted in 1970 showed by 41% to 38% that blacks could 'foresee themselves taking real control of their local government in the next few years' (*Time* 6 April 1970: 19). The largely pessimistic 1971 'State of the Cities' report by the National Urban Coalition has one hopeful note, a 'new tough pride, self-confidence and determination' of minority groups to build up their own self-help organisations and reach 'for the levers of power' (*Time* 11 October 1971: 32).

The black struggle has become localised. The mass movements of the first half of the '60s have largely been replaced by self-help, grass-roots institutions within particular communities and cities. On a variety of fronts, local groups, all ascribing to a basic philosophy of black unity, economic and political power and self-determination, are developing their own organisations (Gerlach and Hine 1970: 390). In the rural South, black co-operatives such as the Mississippi Poor People's Corporation and the Southwest Alabama Farmers Cooperative are springing up. In the North, Detroit's first black-operated bank, the First Independence National Bank, pledged to serve the black community, began in 1970. James Brown has set an example for black capitalists. In 1971 he owned five radio stations. Among his businesses is 'James Brown Golden Platter Restaurants', a chain of restaurants selling soul food. In 1971, Chicago saw the opening, with soul singers in attendance, of Black Expo, a five-day trade fair featuring the products of nearly 400 black firms. With the support of black businessmen, Jackson articulated Black Expo's policy: 'We do not want a welfare state. We have potential. We can produce. We can feed ourselves.' To realise this potential, Jackson proposed a 'domestic Marshall Plan' for black neighbourhoods (*Time* 11 October 1971: 36).

The 1970 opinion poll shows the direction of black perspectives: 77% to 14% believe that 'only militancy, black pride and black unity will compensate for decreasing white support.' The emphasis on self-improvement and on black economic and political power is clearly seen from the response to the question of how blacks will make 'real progress': 97% said by getting more blacks better educated, 93% by starting more black-owned businesses, 92% by electing more blacks to public office (*Time* 6 April 1970: 19).

Over page: Oakland, Miss., June 1966: a marcher points to the KKK painted on the highway, as the Meredith March continues on its way to Jackson. On the right of the front row of marchers is CORE director Floyd McKissick.

Black Identity

Dr Luther Gerlach, who has conducted an important study of the Black Power Movement, writes, 'Participation in the movement is based on the experience of "having soul". There are no objective requirements for membership, and soul brothers recognize each other through a bond of subjectively perceived commitment' (Gerlach and Hine 1970: 392). Soul as a concept, though having some currency before the mid-'60s, greatly expanded its frame of reference and became more widespread after that date. Reflecting and encouraging black pride, soul is an important psychological component of the black struggle. It is a diffuse, almost mystical concept and its emphasis on subjective qualities—'you have to feel it'—encourages emotional commitment to it. As well as having important psychological functions, soul has a sociological role. Its diffuseness allows all black Americans to identify and associate with it and so with each other. As Enoch Gregory (WWRL) says, 'If you got a hundred guys in a room and asked them exactly what soul means, you'll get a hundred and fifty different answers.' Because soul remains largely undefined, in fact it defies definition, all blacks are able to relate to its general mystique. As a symbol, soul unites black organisations which are often fragmentary and based upon varying ideologies. By symbolising the unity of all blacks, it helps them to identify with a common cause. The social differentiation of black society is at least symbolically negated, for soul defines as similar members of a sociologically disparate group (Hannerz 1968: 61). With soul a big city mayor and his lowliest supporter have a common bond. In his election address, Mayor Kenneth Gibson of Newark announced to a crowd of largely black supporters, 'The man who founded Newark over 300 years ago, when he came here, I'm sure, and I'm sure you'll recognise, that he never realized that some day Newark would have soul' (ITV 1971). He thus included every black person in Newark in his victory.

Black pride was an important factor in the ghetto riots of the '60s. The US Riot Commission characterises the 'typical rioter' as extremely proud of being black, but finds it impossible to determine whether this attitude preceded or antedated the riot. The Commission concludes, 'Certainly the riot experience seems to have been associated with increased pride in the minds of many participants.' (National Advisory Commission 1968: 133). The Watts riot was followed by an outburst of black pride reflected in the annual Watts festival commemorating the riot and featuring black cultural achievements. As one Watts resident said in 1967, 'Now the only time you see a process is on the head of a pimp, and even some of the pimps are going "natural" ' (*Newsweek* 7 August 1967: 32). In Watts as in other ghettoes, groups concerned with the teaching and development of black history and black culture have sprung up. Black history is redefined and re-evaluated from today's perspectives. High schools in ghetto areas are developing courses on black culture, and in colleges and universities black study departments are being created to meet the demands of black students.

Soul music plays a vital part in this process. The 1972 Watts Summer Festival closed with 'Wattstax', a seven hour show sponsored by Stax Records and Schlitz Beer, with the proceeds going to black charities. Over 100,000 people watch a parade of soul singers, including the Staple Singers, the Soul Children, Rufus and Carla Thomas and Isaac Hayes. Kim Weston sings the 'Black National Anthem' *Lift Every Voice and Sing*, and the audience jumps to its feet and responds with the black power salute. As he has done in cities across America, the Rev. Jesse Jackson leads the audience in the 'Black Litany'. He announces, 'I am somebody' and they respond, 'I am somebody;' he asks, 'What time is it?' and they reply 'Nation time.' He conducts the final blessing and the people of Watts bow their heads and join hands affirming black pride and unity.

Black identity is being defined by blacks for blacks. Jay Butler (WCHB) outlines his view of the developing black self-concept, relating it to blues and soul music.

> Back in 1954, the black community didn't want to be associated with blues. This was because the civil rights bill had passed and at that time more blacks were wearing processes and using Ultra Skin Tone Cream to try and lighten their complexion, because they wanted to be accepted by whites. But it's since changed. The black community wants to be accepted as black Americans. I don't wanna be a white American, I wanna be a black American. It's like the Detroit Emeralds' song (*I'm An Ordinary Man*) *Take Me The Way I Am*. There's a two fold meaning in all these soul songs. Take Solomon Burke's *Take Me As I Am*. This song might be about a guy and his girl, but it means more at this period of time. Back in the 1950s we were trying to be accepted by white Americans on their terms. Now accept me as I am, accept my nappy hair, accept me period.

Lee Garrett (WGPR) gives a personal account of this transformation of identity.

> When I went to school, I went with mostly white kids, therefore I was kind of brainwashed into hillbilly music, and the white way of thinking and the white way of living, but yet there was still something underneath. When I was small, I wanted to be white y'see, yet there was something missing and I couldn't figure out what it was ... And then I finally realised, I'm not this, I'm black. And though the feeling never left me, it had been hidden so I brought it out.

Right, top: *Rev. Jesse Jackson* (left) *and Al Bell, Executive Vice-President of Stax Records, during* Lift Every Voice And Sing *at Wattstax '71.* Bottom: *Isaac Hayes* (left) *and Rufus Thomas perform at Wattstax '71.*

Enoch Gregory (**WWRL**) explains how this feeling is expressed in behaviour,

> Then [in the late '50s and early '60s], I spoke more standard American, a lot less of the soul vernacular than I do today . . . It's a funny thing that's happened to me. I don't know but it's groovy, whatever it is. As the cat says, 'I'm black and I'm proud.'

The widespread acceptance of soul and the creation of a specifically black identity developed with black power. From the mid-'60s black spokesmen have advocated the indivisibility of black pride and black progress. Pride in blackness transcends class boundaries. *Ebony*, a black version of *Life* magazine with a solid black middle-class readership, has traditionally played down blackness and emphasised middle-class respectability. Its advertisements have featured models with virtually white complexions and features dressed in ultra-conservative clothes. In the late '60s its models grew darker and its perspective increasingly favourable to blackness. In 1969 an *Ebony* editorial reads,

> Negroes, black, Afro-American, coloreds—whatever you might have once called them—today have more of a sense of oneness than ever before . . . I am not ashamed of my color. I'm not ashamed of myself. Like James Brown, I can say, 'Say it loud, I'm black and I'm proud' . . . The constant acceptance of 'white is right' is out. Black people are finding a freedom that they never had before—the freedom to be themselves. (*Ebony* August 1969: 42)

These sentiments are classless.

A specifically black self-concept was encouraged by the fact that, despite definition under the law as Americans, blacks were still defined, at least in terms of residential association, as black and therefore unacceptable as neighbours, by white Americans. The 1970 US census shows that residential segregation increased significantly during the decade 1960-70. This is not due primarily to white exodus from central cities to the suburbs. Residential segregation is also increasing in the suburbs. Nor is it due to a desire on the part of blacks to live amongst themselves. The 1969 poll reveals that 74% of blacks would prefer to live in integrated neighbourhoods (*Newsweek* 30 June 1969: 20). Nor is it a function of black poverty. Studies have shown clearly that this residence pattern is due primarily to white discrimination against blacks (Franklin and Starr 1967: 480-2). Black Americans were not accepted simply as Americans as they had been defined under the law. The 'black and white together' days of the 1963 march on Washington were not fulfilled. Classified as black by the wider society, black Americans created a positive definition of blackness.

Black identity stems primarily from the acceptance and realisation that the destiny of black Americans is in their own hands. Black initiative and self-help, increasing self-confidence and sense of direction, the perception of a collective destiny and the need for unity, created and was reinforced by a definition of blackness that has become a part of black American culture.

Hope: Progress and the Future

The situation in black ghettoes, the social disorganisation and the urban decay, have been amply chronicled (Clark 1965; Liebow 1967; Hannerz 1969; Rainwater 1970). The ghetto can easily be envisaged as a context for fostering blues in terms of both a state of mind and music. But moving from the objective situation to what people feel about it, we may ask: do most black Americans feel they are making progress and do they feel that things will get better? The 1969 Gallup Poll shows that a significant majority believe they have made important gains and will continue to do so: 70% 'say that blacks have made progress in the last five years and an almost equal number believe they will be better off five years from now' (*Newsweek* 30 June 1969: 19). This poll shows more optimism than any previous one. Figure 1 illustrates the growing belief that progress is being made. Soul songs such as *Hope For The Future* and *Push on Jessie Jackson* reflect and encourage this belief.

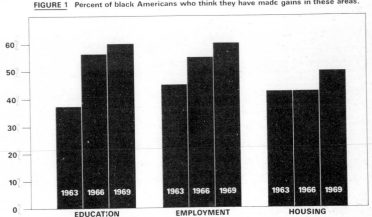

FIGURE 1 Percent of black Americans who think they have made gains in these areas.

Adapted from Newsweek *22 August 1966: 22; 30 June 1969: 19.*

Blues and Black Society

Against the background of this chapter we shall first reconsider ethnicity as a factor in the decline of blues. According to this argument, blues was rejected by large numbers of black Americans because of its ethnic associations. Several informants state that many blacks saw the legal definition of their status in 1954 as an opportunity to rid themselves of the negative stereotypes that had been traditionally associated with blackness. They wanted to be accepted and enter into the mainstream of society simply as Americans. In order to facilitate this process many did their best to act and appear like white Americans, rejecting the more obvious aspects of black culture, one of which was blues. The old maxim that 'white is right' was emphasised still further. This argument could still explain the continuing decline of blues despite the positive definition of blackness in the mid-'60s. After blues' long spell in the musical wilderness, many blacks, particularly younger ones, could have developed tastes for other forms of music. This argument is backed only by retrospective statements of a few informants. Further research is necessary to assess the importance of a rejection of blues on ethnic grounds, as a factor in the decline of the music.

Whatever the virtues of the above thesis, we have argued that a stronger case can be made for the decline of blues. If, as suggested, the primary function of blues is as a vehicle for adaptation to the Jim Crow system, we should expect the music and the system to decline together. We note, beginning in 1955, a significant decline in the number of blues recordings (see Figure 2). That year saw the advent of mass black protest against Jim Crow and the beginning of the end of the system. The actions of black people from the mid-'50s onwards reveal an increasing contradiction of the attitudes and strategies of accommodation and acceptance found in blues. The hurt and frustration produced by the system and the inability to act against it had been turned inward and relieved and released in blues. Now these feelings are increasingly turned outward against the system and blues is no longer required to perform its traditional function. Black Americans are taking their destiny into their own hands and shaping events rather than being shaped by them. The philosophy of blues, accept the situation and make the best of it, struggle on in the face of the inevitable taking what comes, is increasingly rejected. The definition of the situation presented by blues may find reflection in the poorer areas of black ghettoes, but it certainly no longer represents the definition of the future. The majority of blacks believe they have progressed and will progress and have faith in progress itself. Whereas blues advocates living with the situation, black Americans are increasingly determined to change that situation. The growing emphasis upon self- and collective improvement finds little harmony with the 'down in the alley' themes and associations of blues. The developing black pride of the '60s and '70s has little in common with the definition of blackness spelt out in some blues and implied in many more.

From 1940 to 1970 there is ample evidence of economic hardship, a situation which blues had in part been adapted to, and could in theory still respond to. From 1940 to 1954 the economic position of blacks improved at a faster rate and to a greater degree, both in absolute terms and relative to whites, than in any future period (Killingsworth 1969: 204). In theory this reduction in hardship should lead to a reduction of blues, in practice it did not. From 1955 to 1965, while in absolute terms black income rose, relative to white income it remained static and in most years was lower than in 1955. One would expect an increase of blues as a response to this relative deprivation. In fact just the opposite happened. Not until 1966 did black income again begin to rise steadily both in absolute terms and relative to white income. To take a further indicator of economic hardship, unemployment rates, we again find that the predicted relationship between blues and hardship fails to appear (see Figure 2). During the period 1949 to 1969 the six years form 1958 to 1963 reveal significantly higher rates of non-white unemployment (Bureau of Labor Statistics 1970: 29). However, the decline of blues continued during these years.

FIGURE 2

Unemployment rates, relative income, blues records

DATE	Non-white unemployment rate	Non-white relative income	Number of blues records
1950	9·0	54	270
51	5·3	53	310
52	5·4	57	270
53	4·5	56	220
54	9·9	56	230
55	8·7	55	150
56	8·3	53	120
57	7·9	54	160
58	12·6	51	100
59	10·7	52	110
1960	10·2	55	140
61	12·4	53	140
62	10·9	53	110
63	10·8	53	70
64	9·6	56	80
65	8·1	55	80
66	7·3	60	90

The unemployment rate is the percent unemployed in the civilian labour force. Relative income is the median income of non-white families as a percent of white family income. (Source: Bureau of Labor Statistics 1970: 14; 29.)

In conclusion, the decline of blues is primarily a function of the decline of Jim Crow to which the music, and the attitudes and strategies it presented, was adapted. Economic hardship alone fails to explain blues.

Rather, it is economic hardship in concert with Jim Crow that produced the situation to which blues was adapted. With the removal of Jim Crow, black Americans have the opportunity to improve their situation, they have cause for hope and optimism. With Jim Crow and its ultimate sanction gone, the barrier so long considered impenetrable has been broken down. Hopes of improvement by migration to Northern ghettoes had in the past been shortlived in the face of the subtler version of Jim Crow that existed in the North. Now, for the first time, black Americans have hopes for sustained improvement. Figure 2 shows that as the black struggle gained momentum there was a corresponding decline in the demand for blues. Blues is embedded in and adapted to a situation that no longer exists.

The Evolution of Soul Music

The evolution of soul music falls into roughly three periods: 1954 to 1960, 1960 to 1964, and 1964 to the present. Charlie Gillett's *The Sound of the City* covers the main points so they will only be touched on here.

From the middle to the late '50s there were two important black styles of music, both appealing mainly to young audiences. One of these, rock 'n' roll, was in many ways similar to the rhythm and blues that preceded it. The records of Larry Williams, Little Richard and to a lesser extent Fats Domino are largely up-tempo twelve-bar blues. A comparison of Amos Milburn's West Coast rhythm and blues style, exemplified in records such as *House Party*, with Larry Williams's rock 'n' roll records such as *Hootchy Koo* and *Short Fat Fanny* reveals many points of similarity—the same basic twelve-bar pattern, a piano style little changed from boogie woogie, similar sax riffs and vocal stylings. Larry Williams's recording career also illustrates a transition from rock and roll to the beginnings of soul music. In 1958 he was still making records—*Bad Boy; She Said Yeah*—in the style of his former hits. By 1959 his recording of *Get Ready* revealed gospel influences in its rhythms and featured a vocal group singing a mixture of pop and gospel harmonies. By the late '50s black rock 'n' roll was largely replaced by its predecessor, rhythm and blues, though in a somewhat different form.

A second major style of mainly teenage music of this period was provided by vocal groups. From the late '40s to the late '50s groups such as The Ravens and The Orioles and later The Moonglows and Flamingos recorded slow sentimental ballads and, to a lesser extent, novelty up-tempo pop songs. This style is interesting because it comes close to the mainstream of white American popular music. Group harmonies owed more to barbershop quartets than gospel or blues. Lead singers used few of the inflections that characterised other forms of black music. Records such as *You Me And The Sea* by The Flamingos could well have been made by The Four Freshmen. Included in groups' repertoires were Tin Pan Alley standards such as *Red Sails In The Sunset, I Only Have Eyes For You*, and *White Christmas.*

A number of factors may have influenced the development of this style. Many of the groups were formed by teenagers who were either born or grew up in Northern and West Coast cities. They lacked the experience of the South shared by many of their parents. With a frame of reference that was urban and adolescent, they rejected 'down home' ways, and were concerned with developing their own 'hip', 'cool' style of speech, manner and dress (Brown 1965; Gillett 1970; 183-94). Since blues- and gospel-based styles were largely Southern in origin and association, the only suitable precedent in black music was the vocal group styles of the Mills Brothers and Ink Spots. They formed the basis from which the new vocal groups developed. Claude Brown, in his autobiography set in Harlem, recalls the impact of The Orioles when they first appeared at the Apollo Theatre. The streets were filled with small groups of teenagers attempting to imitate The Orioles (Brown 1965: 102-3). They had been presented, by their peers, with a new model of hipness to aspire to. Though many of the vocal group songs dealt with adolescent love, they were hardly a mirror of teenage life in urban ghettoes. Their beauty and tenderness contrasted with rather than reflected life. The groups and their songs formed a part of the self-conscious vocabulary of style with which the young identified, to which they aspired, and in terms of its performance, by which they judged themselves and others.

Two further factors may have influenced the origin and development of the vocal group styles. Firstly, the precedent of the financial rewards of the large white audience enjoyed by the Mills Brothers and Ink Spots. Though supported almost entirely by black audiences in the '40s, the less ethnic-sounding groups, such as the Orioles, Crows and Penguins, broke through to white audiences in the early and mid-'50s (Millar 1971: 32-3). Secondly, this was a time when status considerations based on the 'white is right' principle carried more weight. Bobby Bland's remarks on white vocal groups show something of this attitude, 'The Hi-Los and The Four Freshmen have some blues in their songs. But it's an upper crust blues tune. They put a little class into it.'

Throughout this period (1954-60) and into the early '60s, gospel singing techniques were used by some singers within the framework of popular songs. Artists such as Clyde McPhatter, Sam Cooke, and Jackie Wilson used gospel vocal stylings against a background of pop harmonies and arrangements. Aimed mainly at a young audience, their songs were often bouncy novelty items or sentimental ballads. The beginnings of soul music were apparent in the work of particular singers. Ray Charles made *I Got A Woman* in 1954, *This Little Girl Of Mine* in 1955 and *What'd I Say* in 1959. James Brown made his first record and million-seller, *Please, Please, Please* in 1956. These records were the work of individuals rather than part of an established style.

The period from 1960 to 1964 represents a melting pot of styles, with an increasing use of gospel techniques. The decline of black rock 'n' roll brought a return of rhythm and blues in a modified form; gospel singing styles were often used within a twelve-bar blues framework. Bobby Parker's *Watch Your Step* (1961) is a good example of this approach, and James Brown's *Shout And Shimmy* (1962) carries gospel techniques even further. Records began to appear using chord progressions and harmonies from gospel music, *You Don't Miss Your Water* (1961) by William Bell and *People Get Ready* (1963) by The Impressions being notable examples. Black vocal groups such as The Isley Brothers and The Falcons began to move away from the vocal group styles of the '50s and *I Found A Love* (1962) by The Falcons (with Wilson Pickett as lead singer) set the tone for much of the soul music that was to follow. Most black informants place the beginnings of soul music as a style (rather than the first soul records) during the period 1960 to 1964. Jeffrey Troy (WWRL), a young disc-jockey, sums up the views of many blacks in their 20s and early 30s:

> I can still listen to the songs of 1960 and after, and still identify these with what's happening today. Whereas beyond that time, generally speaking, I don't like the music, the real oldies, the Olympics, the Clovers, Clyde McPhatter, I can't identify.

By the mid-'60s soul music became established as the major style of black American music. Its audience demanded a style that was unquestionably black, yet not too reminiscent of blues. Soul music, firmly rooted in gospel, probably the oldest unbroken musical tradition in black culture, met these requirements. In January, 1964, King Curtis heralded a new era with *Soul Serenade*. In 1964 and 1965 artists such as Solomon Burke, Otis Redding, Wilson Pickett, Sam and Dave and the Temptations rose to fame, and James Brown was well on the way to becoming Soul Brother Number One.

The evolution of soul music closely parallels the stages in the black movement for civil rights and self-determination. The scattered soul records from 1954 to 1960 correspond to the black struggle during those years which was intermittent and sporadic and never reached the proportions of a mass movement. The convergence of styles towards soul music from 1960 to 1964 corresponds to the protest movements of the early '60s when the civil rights struggle became a mass movement. The establishment of soul music as the dominant style of black musical expression in the mid-'60s correlates with the rise and development of the Black Power Movement.

Soul music reflects, directs and harmonises with the mood of black Americans. Songs like *We're Rolling On* capture the impetus and dynamism of black society. With themes emphasising togetherness, the popularity of soul music transcends the barriers of age and class. With lyrics which articulate the concept of soul and singers who personify

Wilson Pickett.

it, soul music symbolises black self-definition and self-determination. Reflected in the lyrics and form of soul music are the attitudes and strategies, hopes and expectations, of black Americans in the '60s and '70s.

To nearly every black person who contributed to this book, soul music is a synthesis of gospel music and blues. The sacred and the profane have been united. In soul music the antithesis of the styles of life that blues and gospel traditionally represented is denied. The divisions in black society that blues and gospel formerly symbolised have in music been eliminated. Reflected in soul music is the spirit and ideal, if not the reality, of black unity.

Appendix 1/Reality and Response
—The Black Family

The lyrics of blues and soul music deal mainly with the relationships of men and women. Blues is largely concerned with problems within, or breakdowns of, relationships. This content is shared in part by soul music, though its perspective is often more hopeful and constructive. Many soul songs rejoice in the success of relationships and express a determination to maintain and improve them, an outlook that is infrequent in blues. An examination of blues and soul music in association with male-female relationships in black society reveals the basis in social structure for many of the themes of the music.

Statistical data, available from 1950 onwards, show that there has been a steady increase in the breakup of black marriages. This increase is particularly apparent in the lowest income areas: in Cleveland's Hough ghetto, the percentage of families with female heads rose from 23% to 32% from 1960 to 1965; in Watts, Los Angeles, from 36% to 39% for the same period. In the lowest income group, families with under $3,000 a year, the figures for 1968 show that 56% of all black families were headed by women, compared with 27% for white. Overall, the proportion of nonwhite families with both husband and wife present decreased from 77.7% in 1950 to 68.7% in 1969, compared with a slight increase from 88.0% to 88.8% for whites over the same period. Though the statistics indicate that low income is a primary factor in the breakup of marriages, the discrepancy between the proportion of black and white female-headed families in the same income bracket suggests that other factors are also at work. In the highest income category, families with $15,000 and over per annum, the 1968 figures show that 7% of black families are headed by women, compared with 3% for white. The approximately two to one ratio applies to all income brackets.

Low income black ghetto areas are characterised by unstable relationships between the sexes, divorces, separations and impermanent, shifting unions. In general, observers have interpreted this situation as a product of economic factors. Unemployment, underemployment and low pay result in the failure of many men to support their families adequately. In 1967, the proportion of separations or divorces was more than twice as high among unemployed nonwhite men than among the employed. The economic strain is exacerbated by the fact that the average nonwhite poor urban family is larger than its white counterpart, containing 4.8 persons compared with 3.7. A man's job and income effect his standing in domestic and social life. His failure to perform his role adequately as breadwinner diminishes his prestige and authority within the family. Even if he finds employment, many of the jobs available to working class black males are poorly paid, menial in content and low in status. One result of the relationship of black males to the job market is the proportionately high number of black women who go out to work, 57% compared with 45% for whites, in the age group 20 to 44. When the woman is working and bringing money into the household and her husband is unemployed, the man's role as husband and breadwinner is further undermined, a situation that tends to produce conflict within the marriage. The operation of supplementary payments to families with dependent children does nothing to support the man's position within his family. Aid to Families with Dependent Children (AFDC) is paid directly to the mother, thus providing her with an independent source of income. In many areas, a 'man in the house rule' operates. Families with an employable male in the house, whether or not he might be able to find employment, are ineligible for AFDC. Unemployed men may feel, and actually be, a liability to their families, increasing their sense of alienation from their wives and children.

Given the situation outlined above, many men abdicate their responsibilities as husbands and fathers and leave home. The conflict and tensions caused by their inability to fulfill these roles break up the marriage. They move, often to single-room apartments with a radio, record player and those in similar circumstances as their main companions.

A significant factor in assessing relations between men and women is the importance of the male peer group in low income black society. It forms a setting in which self respect is possible, positive self-expression available, a context in which men can feel relatively successful. The strength of the male peer group may well be largely a result of unsatisfactory marital relationships. In any case, it has an important effect upon those relationships. In the company of their fellows, men are concerned with giving the impression, which may or may not have a basis in fact, of numerous successful relationships with women. These range from 'pimping' off women—receiving financial support and sexual favours—to having a large number of female acquaintances. Success with the opposite sex is a source of prestige. Another yardstick for success within the peer group is a man's skill with words. This covers the ability to embroider and embellish events so they become unusual and special in form if not in content, to 'rap' with women to gain their admiration and favour and generally to manipulate the actions of others to one's own ends by skilful verbal tactics. Prestige is also gained from expensive and stylish clothes, which, like the other concerns of the male peer group, enhance the individual and add a touch of drama to his presence. The group's definition of manliness includes an emphasis on toughness in order to command and retain respect and a concern in conversation and in act with the consumption of liquor.

These activities detract from a settled, stable married life: time, money, energy, and loyalties are diverted from the home on to the streets and into the bars, clubs and pool rooms. The status and self-respect that may have been lost in marriage and employment may in part be regained by the successful performance of the male role in the context of the peer group.

Into the institution of marriage men bring an attachment to their peer group which promises some satisfactions and a relationship to the job market which offers few. A stable family life with the man as head of the household, breadwinner and authority figure is considered the ideal and conflict between the spouses results from the comparison of ideal and reality. Many men, finding little satisfaction within marriage, look for gratification outside the home, a situation which leads to quarrels and recrimination. The wife often takes over the running of the household and accepts the responsibility for and authority over her children. With their authority eroded, men often accuse their wives of being dominating and overbearing. Under these circumstances marriages frequently break down. The break-up of marriage usually finds the partners embarking upon transitory, unstable consensual unions. In such relationships the rights and duties of the couple are often ill defined and there is a lack of reciprocity of expectations, factors which impede chances of success. Many separated women set up house with their grandmother and children, and having tried marriage and found it wanting, decide not to try it again. Their needs for male companionship and sex are provided by boy friends who sometimes live under the same roof and contribute financially to the upkeep of the family, but have no real responsibility or authority in the household. Many men have no real homes, drifting from household to household, apartment to apartment.

As important as the reality of the situation are the beliefs, attitudes and expectations which surround it, the cultural assessments of male-female relationships. Both partners have their doubts about the gratifications provided by marriage and its chances of success. Each suspects the other's tendency to be unfaithful. Both sexes often maintain that men are not by inclination monogamous, and the nature of street life at least appears to give ample opportunity for them to indulge their appetites. Women, though not seen to be generally promiscuous, are held to be susceptible to temptation. Women have a low expectation of their husband's ability to provide and men share these doubts. These misgivings surrounding marriage are social currency and predate any experience which may validate them. There is therefore a tendency for the beliefs and expectations surrounding marriage and male-female relationships in low income black areas to become self-fulfilling. (Bureau of Labor Statistics 1970; Clark 1965; Hannerz 1969; Leibow 1967; National Advisory Commission 1968; Rainwater 1965, 1970.)

Detroit, February and March 1971, a run-down apartment building in the ghetto area. Men from their late 20s to early 60s live alone in some twenty bedsitters, paying $70 a month for a sparsely furnished room: a bed, a chair, a threadbare carpet, leaking gas cookers, archaic refrigerators, a heating system that fluctuates randomly through twenty degrees, tattered curtains and roaches. Some of the men are unemployed, some have part time jobs, a few have regular full-time employment. Most are separated from their legal or common law wives, others have never maintained a relationship with the opposite sex for any period of time. Often during the bitter winter evenings they sit in their rooms, alone, or in small groups, listening to B.B. King, Bobby Bland and Z.Z. Hill on the record player and the Top Forty soul songs on the radio. As midnight approaches and whisky bottles and beer cans empty, affirmation of the lyrics grows louder and more frequent. Alcohol intensifies the communion with the music as experiences are related to the lyrics.

From the circumstances of men like these, from their despair and loneliness, from their failure to achieve a lasting and fulfilling relationship with a woman, blues and soul music draws much of its content and power to move the listener. A typical B.B. King performance before a black audience provides illustration.

B.B. begins with the uptempo *Everyday I Have The Blues* which portrays his isolation and despair, a life of worries and troubles in which nobody loves him or seems to care. A slow blues, *Worry, Worry*, depicts his sadness and misery over a relationship which has broken down. The hopelessness of the song is often mitigated by a cautionary monologue,

> I'd like to tell you a little story now.
> Ladies, if you got a man, husband, whatever you want to
>   call him,
> And he don't do exactly like you think he should,
> Don't cut him because you can't raise him up again.
> Don't hurt him, treat him nice.
> And fellas, I wanna say to you,
> If you got a wife, a woman, or whatever you wanna call her,
> (And) She don't do exactly like you think she should,
> Don't go upside her head,
> That don't do but one thing,
> That make her a little smarter
> She won't let you catch her next time.
> So all you do is talk to her softly, real sweet y'know,
> And you tell her,
> I know you'll do better.

The medium-tempo *I'm Gonna Do What They Do To Me* is a response to B.B.'s disillusionment with his former relationships. He asserts that the next woman he gets must have a job and pay the bills. She must stay in her place and raise no objection when he goes out on the town. He admits that this may sound cold and unfair, but he's been hurt so many times that he's past caring. He concludes that if this is the way life has got to be, 'I'm gonna do what they do to me.' *How Blue Can You Get* catalogues the feelings produced by an unsatisfactory relationship. No matter how hard B.B. tries, his woman is continually dissatisfied. In the well known blues *It's My Own Fault* B.B. accepts the blame for the failure of his marriage. His wife gave him love, she worked and brought money home to him, while he spent it on other women. As a result she began seeing other men and threatened to leave him, an outcome which he admits is 'my own fault.' In *Paying The Cost To Be The Boss,* B.B. deals with the problem of the man's authority in the household. His wife ignores him, expects to gratify her every whim, and, to make matters worse, acts as though she is ashamed of him. He asserts that he will drink and play poker if he wants to and won't put up with any sermons about the way he is supposed to live. Since he takes care of her and pays the bills, her behaviour is unjustified, for he is 'paying the cost to be the boss'. If she refuses to comply with his assessment of the situation, she can leave.

Judging from the affirmative responses of the audiences at B.B. King performances, he is dealing with problems and experiences that many share. This is confirmed by his conversations with fans, who wander in for

a chat through the ever-open door of his dressing room. Recalling some of these visits, B.B. states,

> A lot of people come to me with their problems and I try and help 'em straighten them out, and sometimes it seem to me, it helps me with mine. I've had some women that say that the things that I've said was the right thing to make the man understand them. For instance, like they say one of the records I made like *Paying The Cost To Be The Boss*, the woman said if her man have him pay the cost, then he should be the boss. But if he's not payin' the cost, meanin' this, if he's not takin' care of her and she have to work, then she figure that she have just about as much say as he does.

An interesting comparison to B.B. King's treatment of relationships between the sexes is provided by Syl Johnson. A youthful, athletic performer, Syl Johnson uses much the same subject matter as B.B. King, but shapes it to his own personality and stage presence. During *Who's Making Love*, a cautionary tale about infidelity, Syl's arrogance and infectious humour are soon apparent as he delivers a monologue over the band's backing,

> Somebody was lovin' my old lady,
> But I didn't care,
> She was at home makin' love,
> And I was out on the streets makin' love,
> She was happy and I was happy.

The audience is chuckling and Syl is enjoying himself.

> The woman I was with was together
> She had a thing going on like this. Uh!
> And the man that she was with in my house,
> He was standing proud all the time.
> I was happy and she was happy,
> It don't make no difference.

In his own song *Don't Give It Away*, Syl deals with the romance, finance problem, a theme which occurs frequently in both blues and soul music. During the song he delivers a short piece of advice,

> Baby, you better beware now,
> 'Cos romance without finance won't get you nowhere,
> Listen, don't give it away,
> Make 'em all pay.

In another of his own songs *I Take Care Of Homework*, Syl boasts that his wife will remain faithful when he is not at home. He delivers, not without humour, a catalogue of the responsibilities he fulfills as a dutiful husband—mopping the floor, taking out the garbage, taking the clothes to the laundromat, leaving food in the icebox, giving her all his money and taking care of her in sickness and in health. His reward for 'taking care of

homework' is a wife he can trust to remain faithful. (For further aspects of Syl Johnson's performance in this context, see page 108.)

Since this performance in1969, Syl Johnson has followed a general trend in soul music, the celebration of successful relationships, with songs like, *We Do It Together* and *We Did It*.

The relationship between black music, family stability, income and employment raises interesting problems. Comparing statistics on the rates of nonwhite employment, separation rates of married couples and the number of AFDC cases opened, Daniel Moynihan found a close relationship between them. From 1948 to 1962 the nonwhite unemployment rate and the number of AFDC cases opened rose and fell together. However, from 1962 to 1964 they diverged with unemployment going down and the number of AFDC cases rising. Taking nonwhite unemployment and the separation rate of married couples, Moynihan found a similar trend. From 1953 to 1962 the unemployment and separation rates rose and fell together. However a sharp drop in unemployment from 1962 to 1964 was not accompanied by a decrease in the number of broken marriages. Moynihan suggests the possibility that a situation which originally may have been caused by low income and unemployment, has become endemic to certain sections of black society. He concludes,

> It would be troubling indeed to learn that until several years ago, employment opportunity made a great deal of difference in the rate of Negro dependency and family disorganization, but that the

Syl Johnson. Left: *playing at 1304 Rush Street, Chicago, 1960.* Above: *a more recent publicity photograph, for Twinight Records.*

situation has so deteriorated that the problem is now feeding on itself . . . (Moynihan 1965: 134-59)

Extending the time span covered by Moynihan's data, and adding two new indices, we discover that the trend indicated by his figures is continuing. From 1950 until the early '60s there is a close relationship between social and economic factors suggesting causal interrelationships. However, from the early '60s, with unemployment falling and the median income gap between white and nonwhite decreasing, separations of husband and wife due to marital discord and the number of families with a female head are increasing.

From these indications, an increase in the popularity of blues might be predicted. The opposite has occurred. An increase in the number of soul songs expressing sorrow over broken relationships might be expected, but again, it appears that this is not the case. What has occurred, as noted in

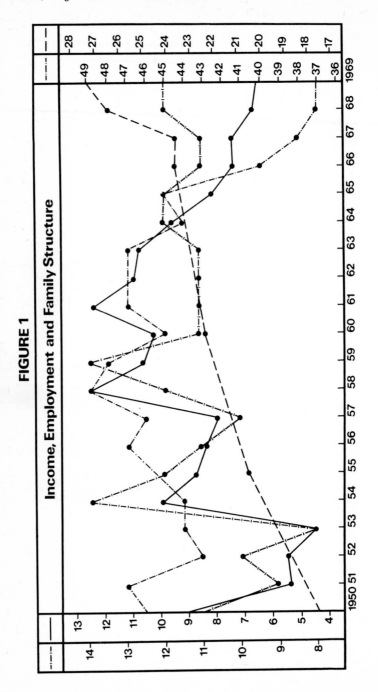

FIGURE 1

Income, Employment and Family Structure

Chapter 3, is an increase in soul music of themes expressing a determination to maintain and improve relationships, an advocacy of standard marital roles as the ideal and a celebration of their successful translation into action and a general perspective of hope and optimism in regard to relations between men and women. These themes appear to contradict the situation as portrayed by the statistical data. It is possible that there is, despite the worsening reality of the situation, a determination that was previously lacking, to improve it, and an emerging belief in the efficacy of effort.

KEY TO FIGURE 1 (opposite)

_____ *Non-white unemployment rate (the unemployment rate is the percent unemployed in the civilian labour force).*

—.—. *Percentage difference between median income of non-white and white families.*

—ı—ı *Percent of non-white ever-married women not living with their husbands because of marital discord.*

_ _ _ *Percent of non-white families with a female head (annual figures available only from 1966 onwards).*

(Compiled from data in Bureau of Labor Statistics, 1970).

Appendix 2/Counter-Thesis

The argument throughout this book has seen society as the primary determinant of the form of music. General trends in music and society have been examined, and causal relationships posited between those trends. The thesis has been presented in general terms which, to a degree, have glossed over the complexity of the situation. It has been stated that blues has, and to some extent still does, find its main support from the poorest and least educated sections of black society. There are exceptions to this generalisation. E. Rodney Jones is a senior disc-jockey at WVON, Chicago's foremost black radio station. Middle class in terms of income, a self-made, successful man, committed to black progress, one time president of NATRA, the mainly black National Association of Television and Radio Announcers, E. Rodney Jones is a staunch supporter of blues. He maintains this support at a time when blues is steadily decreasing in popularity. When WVON gives disc-jockeys the occasional opportunity to play blues, Rodney Jones takes full advantage of it. Should audience tastes permit, he would like to play more blues on his programmes. The generalisations advanced about the 'average blues fan' would not cover the case of E. Rodney Jones.

Ralph Ellison in his critique of Leroi Jones's *Blues People* gives an eloquent warning of the dangers of placing too much confidence in the predictive power of generalisations.

> One would get the impression that there was a rigid correlation between color, education, income and the Negro's preference in music. But what are we to say of a white-skinned Negro with brown freckles who owns sixteen oil wells sunk in a piece of Texas land once farmed by his ex-slave parents who were a blue-eyed, white-skinned, red-headed (kinky) Negro woman from Virginia and a blue-gummed, black-skinned, curly-haired Negro male from Mississippi, and who not only sang bass in a Holy Roller church, played the market and voted Republican, but collected blues recordings and was a walking depository of blues tradition? (Ellison 1966: 245)

Two points arise from Ellison's caution. Firstly, if we accept our major thesis as valid, then the exceptions to it must be accounted for. It appears that some people enjoy music either despite their particular circumstances and the general state of society, or because that music exists for them largely in isolation from these factors. Thus, whatever the general trends in music and society, some people like a particular style of music because they like it—they simply follow their aesthetic sensibilities which override or are unaffected by other considerations. Following our thesis and the evidence presented, it is argued that such people are the exception rather than the rule.

A second point deriving from Ellison's warning could, if valid, contradict our thesis. If the exceptions are motivated in their choice of music simply by aesthetic considerations, why not everybody? This position would maintain that the relationships between music and society advanced in this book are coincidental rather than causal. It would suggest that music operates as a closed system, obeying its own rules and developing from its own premises. An examination of this position with regard to blacks and country and western music shows that it does not stand up against the evidence.

Before 1950, black Americans in the Southern states heard little other than country and western on the radio. With this exposure to the music, it would be reasonable to expect, all things being equal, a large black following for country and western music. Bobby Bland recalls,

> I used to listen to the radio every morning to people like Gene Steer, Roy Acuff, Lefty Frizzell, Hank Williams, Hank Snow. I think hillbilly has more of a story than the people give them credit for y'know, because they have some real strong lyrics. We were taught that hillbilly wasn't the thing, but I guarantee you they were wrong.

If music were unrelated to social factors, why the partisan nature of musical appreciation which Bobby Bland refers to? Given the exposure of black Americans to country music, why is it absent from record shops catering to a black public? Why are there no black country and western singers performing to black audiences? At least one soul singer, Joe Simon, would like to sing country and western songs, but is unable to find a black audience for the music and believes his colour prevents him from acceptance by a white country audience. He states, 'I like country music. I'd sing country, but in order to be successful, I guess I'd have to change my colour' (*R 'n' B World* 17 October 1968: 5). O.B. McClinton, one of the very few black country and western singers, has had to struggle against the prejudices of his own people. Born in Senatobia, Mississippi, he states, 'I grew up listening to Grand Ole Opry and was brought up believing that only white folks sang country and western until I was nearly grown.' He had to put up with such disparaging epithets as 'black country boy' and 'black hillbilly'. He explains some of the difficulties he has tried to overcome,

> Black people have never been identified with country music simply because the music has always been identified with hillbillies and there are no black hillbillies. Some blacks enjoy listening to country music but feel that they can't sing it from stage. A lot of them feel that it is just 'out of their place' to sing it. (Stax Public Relations (2) n.d.)

We return, therefore, to support our original thesis. Musical form is primarily a product of the nature of society. Using the example of country and western music, the exception again highlights the rule. One of the biggest sellers in the country and western market, Charley Pride, is black. His unique position has resulted in considerable publicity from the media. He says, 'Why I sing country music is simple to answer—I like it. I heard a musical sound that I liked when I was a kid and that sound just happened to be known as country' (*Melody Maker* 27 May 1972: 19). Despite the probability that many blacks have shared Charley Pride's childhood experience, only a handful have crossed the racial divide in terms of their music and audience.

There is a further argument, which, if valid, would modify our thesis. It states that it is merely the coincidence of time and place that relates music to society. The listener associates a particular form of music with the nature of society at a particular time, simply because the music happened to be current at that time. Thus when Chuck Berry introduces a slow blues with the words 'Can't play too many of those blues 'cos it gets to you and you gets to thinkin' of those olden days in south America' (BBC-TV 2, 22 July 1972, 'Sounds For Saturday'), he is reminded of Jim Crow merely because the music and the system are contemporaneous. This argument would accept that events outside music would affect that music. It would state that blues was rejected because it brought back memories of a system which is rapidly disappearing and which few wish to be reminded of. However, it would say nothing more. It would not explain, for example, why gospel music in particular became the basis for soul in the '60s and '70s. It would say only that a form of music, differing from blues, would become the music of that era. Only by positing a closer relationship of music and society can we explain the origins and development of soul music. The argument that relates society and music solely on grounds of contemporaneity, and the associations that the listener draws from that fact, is therefore inadequate. It forms only a part of the wider thesis presented in the body of the book.

Appendix 3/The Future

As blues ceases to play its traditional role in black society, as its committed audience disappears and it dies as a vital part of everyday experience, it will, paradoxically, gain a new and very different kind of acceptance. This will be made possible by blues losing its former social functions, and the passage of time erasing its negative associations. Acceptance will be based on a new definition of the music, blues as art, folklore and tradition. Significantly, this modified support will come first, if not primarily, from those sections of black society least committed to blues in the past. If singer Diahann Carroll's statement has general application, the black middle class is beginning to accept the music it formerly rejected.

> When I was young, middle class Negro parents always told their children to avoid that terrible music called the blues. It was something out of the past that lacked dignity and should be ignored. Today, American culture recognizes the blues as part of our people's heritage. Even more ironic is the fact that black families now find it proper to encourage their children to participate in this musical revival. (*Blues Unlimited* 84: 17)

The Washington Blues Festival held in November 1970 was the first blues festival produced by blacks for blacks. According to the press handout it was, 'an attempt to return blues to the black community given that many white interests have exploited the music at the expense of many of the black musicians who will be performing . . .' (*Blues Unlimited* 78: 15). Again, the disproportionate support of past and present is evident. Of all the cities with large black populations, Washington is probably the one which traditionally has had the least commitment to blues.

Since the emergence of Little Johnny Taylor in 1963 with his best-selling *Part Time Love*, no new blues singer has achieved a significant black following. Two relatively new young blues singers, Taj Mahal and Larry Johnson, have been successful, though primarily with white audiences. Their repertoires consist largely of recreations of old country blues which the passage of time and the circumstances of their original performers have glossed with the aura of folklore.

In these circumstances it is probable that blues will eventually die out in black America. With an occasional conscious resurrection and an evaluation as folklore, it will become too detached to retain its vitality and directness.

The present climate of American society has produced the largest white market to date for the products of black entertainers. Soul singers are

featured on major television shows, and their records sell in ever increasing quantities in the white market. Film scores are written and performed by top soul artists—Isaac Hayes composed and performed the music for *Shaft*, Curtis Mayfield for *Superfly*, Marvin Gaye for *Trouble Man*, Bobby Womack for *Across 110th Street* and James Brown for *Black Caesar*. Soul music is rapidly becoming a part of the mainstream of the entertainment media. Its future as a distinctive form of black American music is in doubt, as singers will become increasingly conscious of the tastes of their white audience. A case in point is the future of soul artists who have composed film music. To date, the films they have scored have dealt with aspects of black society and the music has reflected this. However if they were commissioned to write the music for films covering a variety of subjects, their music might well change, and this change could effect the whole of soul music.

Above: *recognition from the black establishment: B.B. King receives the keys of the city of Cleveland from Mayor Carl B. Stokes.* Right: *Isaac Hayes is honoured for* Theme from *Shaft* Top left: *Academy Award for 'Best Song of the Year';* right, *the Dr Martin Luther King Jr Nobel Peace Prize Replica from the Milwaukee Chapter of Operation Breadbasket;* bottom, *the 1971 NAACP Image Award, at the Beverly Hilton, Beverly Hills, Ca. Others receiving awards for* Shaft *are (*left to right*) Joel Freeman, Gordon Parks and Richard Roundtree.*

Above and right: *Curtis Mayfield.*

Black singers wish to reach the white market for financial and for less objective reasons. Summarising part of an interview held in 1969 with Curtis Mayfield, reporter Judy Spiegelman notes his response to lack of support from the white audience,

> He has been slighted in spirit. His desire is to reach as wide and varied an audience as possible with his message and he is concerned with his inability to do this. As with many black performers who wish to break into the pop mainstream, Mayfield feels that his failure so far has been his own fault. He finds himself attempting to alter his music to please the white audience, since he presumes that the white audience hasn't appreciated his music up to this point because the music has been wrong. (*Soul* 22 September 1969: 17)

Since this interview Curtis Mayfield has changed his music, in part by introducing aspects of white progressive music. He now has a large white following while still retaining his black audience. However a modification of soul music in the direction of white music is not always necessary for white support. When James Brown plays in downtown auditoriums away from the ghetto areas, he attracts large numbers of whites. Yet his act is little changed from the Apollo or the Regal. Despite the fact that in 1972 James Brown's records began to appear with 'The brand new pop sound' printed on the label, his music has made no apparent concessions to white tastes. The description is merely a new definition of an old product.

Because of growing white acceptance, black singers and musicians are becoming less dependent on black audiences. A larger and more varied following allows them greater freedom in their choice of music. They can more easily follow their musical inclinations rather than being forced to cater to the tastes of a limited audience. Stevie Wonder provides an example of this process. His albums 'Where I'm Coming From', 'Music Of My Mind' and 'Talking Book' reveal a strong influence of white progressive pop music, and as a result he has become a major attraction in the white market. He notes the response of a black audience when he first introduced this type of material into his stage act,

> I played the Apollo in New York last week and most of the people who saw the show didn't understand what I was doing. From their reaction it seemed like they thought I'd gone crazy. They couldn't believe how unlike Motown the act was. But I'm not trying to be different; I'm just trying to be myself. (*Disc and Music Echo* 15 January, 1972: 10)

Despite this initial reaction, Stevie Wonder's albums have strong sales in the black market. This suggests that if sounds from outside the framework of soul music are incorporated into it, and presented by a singer with whom the black audience can identify, the music will be accepted. Yet Stevie Wonder has still to regain his black audience in the Southern states where tastes are closer to the mainstream of soul music. In 1973 he states, 'But in the South, it seems like people don't come out to see me, and in those big halls, well it really sounds bad when they're empty.' (*Melody Maker* 10 February 1973: 17).

Turning to our major thesis, the integral relationship of music and society, it follows that it is necessary to predict the future of black American society in order to predict the course of black music. If black society becomes integrated into the mainstream of white America, if the black experience ceases to be particular and the problems and concerns of black and white are shared, then it follows that black music will largely cease to be a distinctive entity. Those aspects which remain distinctive will be a product of the past rather than being fashioned by the present. Already this process is apparent in some aspects of soul music and it may possibly presage changes in the structure of American society. An increasing number of black singers, such as Bill Withers, Roberta Flack and The 5th Dimension, are no longer distinctively ethnic, and in appealing to a white public also retain a black following. Bill Withers states, 'One of the biggest pleasures that I have had so far is that old people, young people, black people and white people have been able to relate to what I have been doing' (*Melody Maker* 6 May 1972: 47). A similar process is evident from the themes of soul music. Preoccupied during the middle and late '60s with black self-determination, Curtis Mayfield's songs are now concerned more with love, peace and pollution, subjects which transcend racial barriers. The changing style of his music may well reflect these new concerns. Harvey Fuqua, who has played an active role in black music for over twenty years as singer, songwriter, manager and record producer, gives his assessment of the overall situation of popular music, 'Everybody's playing music now. People are playing whatever they want to play and they're listening to whatever they want to listen to, and I think it's great. It's all coming together' (*Melody Maker* 18 March 1972: 29). Only time will tell whether these observations will ever apply to society in general.

Bibliography

Agricultural Economic Report No. 170, *Human Resources in the Mississippi Delta*. U.S. Government Printing Office, Washington D.C., 1970.

Bureau of Labor Statistics Report No. 375, *The Social and Economic Status of Negroes in the United States, 1969*. U.S. Government Printing Office, Washington D.C., 1970.

BAGDIKIAN, Ben H. 'The Black Immigrants' in *The Saturday Evening Post*, 15 July 1967.

BEALE, Calvin L. 'The Negro in American Agriculture', in *The American Negro Reference Book*, edited by John P. Davis, Prentice Hall, Englewood Cliffs, 1966.

BROWN, Claude. *Manchild In The Promised Land*. Signet Books, New York, 1965.

BRUYNOGHE, Yannick. *Big Bill Blues*. Oak Publications, New York, 1964.

CARMICHAEL, Stokely and HAMILTON, Charles V. *Black Power*. Penguin Books, Harmondsworth, 1969.

CHARTERS, Samuel B. *The Poetry of the Blues*. Oak Publications, New York, 1963.

CHARTERS, Samuel B. *The Bluesmen*. Oak Publications, New York, 1967.

CLARK, Kenneth. *Dark Ghetto*. Harper and Row, New York, 1965.

COURLANDER, Harold. *Negro Folk Music, U.S.A.* Columbia University Press, New York, 1963.

CRAMER, Alex. 'Goin' to Chicago' in *Coda* 9: 12 (March/April 1971).

DAVIS, Allison, GARDNER, Burleigh B., and GARDNER, Mary R. *Deep South*. Phoenix Books, The University of Chicago Press, Chicago, 1965.

DIXON, Robert M.W., and GODRICH, John. *Recording The Blues*. Studio Vista, London, 1970.

ELLISON, Ralph. *Shadow And Act*. Signet Books, New York, 1964.

FRANKLIN, John Hope and STARR, Isidore. *The Negro in Twentieth Century America*. Vintage Books, Random House, New York, 1967.

FRAZIER, E. Franklin. *The Negro Church in America*. Schocken Books, New York, 1963.

GARLAND, Phyl. *The Sound of Soul*. Henry Regnery Company, Chicago, 1969.

GERLACH, Luther P. and HINE, Virginia H. *'The Social Organisation of a Movement of Revolutionary Change: Case Study, Black Power',* in *Afro-American Anthropology,* edited by Norman E. Whitten Jr. and John F. Szwed, The Free Press, New York, 1970.

GILLETT, Charlie. *The Sound of the City.* Outerbridge & Dienstfrey, New York, 1970; Souvenir Press, London, 1971.

GODRICH, John and DIXON, Robert M.W. *Blues and Gospel Records 1902-1942.* Storyville Publications, London, 1969.

GREVATT, Ren. Sleeve notes to 'What'd I Say/Ray Charles' (London HA-E 2226), n.d.

HANNERZ, Ulf. 'What Negroes Mean By "Soul",' *Transaction* 5:8.

HANNERZ, Ulf. *Soulside: Inquiries into Ghetto Culture and Community.* Columbia University Press, New York, 1969.

HARALAMBOS, Michael. 'Soul Music and Blues: Their Meaning and Relevance in Northern United States Black Ghettoes', in *Afro-American Anthropology,* edited by Norman E. Whitten Jr., and John F. Szwed, The Free Press, New York, 1970.

HEILBUT, Tony. *The Gospel Sound: Good News And Bad Times.* Simon and Schuster, New York, 1971.

JOHNSON, Charles S. *Shadow of the Plantation.* The University of Chicago Press, Chicago, 1934.

KARPE, Kenneth Lee. Sleeve notes to 'Ray Charles at Newport' (London LTZ-K 15149), n.d.

KEIL, Charles. *Urban Blues.* The University of Chicago Press, Chicago, 1966.

KILLINGSWORTH, Charles C. 'Jobs and Income for Negroes', in *Race and the Social Sciences,* edited by Irwin Katz and Patricia Gurin, Basic Books, New York, 1969.

LEADBITTER, Mike, and SLAVEN, Neil. *Blues Records: 1943-1966.* Hanover Books, London, 1968.

LIEBOW, Elliot. *Tally's Corner.* Little, Brown and Company, Boston, 1967.

MILLAR, Bill. *The Drifters.* Studio Vista, London, 1971.

MOYNIHAN, Daniel Patrick. 'Employment, Income, And The Ordeal Of The Negro Family' in *The Negro American,* edited by Talcott Parsons and Kenneth B. Clark, Houghton Mifflin Company, Boston, 1965.

National Advisory Commission. *Report of the National Advisory Commission on Civil Disorders.* Bantam Books, New York, 1968.

OLIVER, Paul. *The Meaning of the Blues.* Collier Books, New York, 1963. (Originally published as *Blues Fell This Morning.*)

OLIVER, Paul. *Conversation with the Blues.* Cassell, London, 1965.

OLIVER, Paul. *Screening the Blues.* Cassell, London, 1968.

OLIVER, Paul. *The Story Of The Blues.* Barrie & Rockcliff, The Cresset Press, London, 1969.

OLIVER, Paul. 'Bill Williams' in *Jazz and Blues* 1: 5 (August/September 1971).

PHIFER, Edward W. 'Slavery in Microcosm: Burke County, North Carolina', in *American Negro Slavery*, edited by Allen Weinstein and Frank Otto Gatell, Oxford University Press, New York and London, 1968.

The Pulse Inc. (1) *Detroit City Michigan, Negro Audience, February-March, 1968.*
(2) *New York City Five County Survey Area, Negro Radio Audience, January to April, 1968.*

RAINWATER, Lee. *Behind Ghetto Walls.* Aldine, Chicago, 1970.

RAINWATER, Lee. 'Crucible Of Identity: The Negro Lower-Class Family', in *The Negro American*, edited by Talcott Parsons and Kenneth B. Clark, Houghton Mifflin Company, Boston, 1965.

SEGAL, Ronald. *The Race War.* Penguin Books, Harmondsworth, 1967.

Stax Public Relations (1) *Little Sonny.* Stax Records, Memphis, n.d.
(2) *O.B. McClinton, The Black Country Irishman!* Stax Records, Memphis, n.d.

TAEUBER, Karl E. 'Negro Population and Housing: Demographic Aspects of a Social Accounting Scheme', in *Race and the Social Sciences*, edited by Irwin Katz and Patricia Gurin, Basic Books, New York, 1969.

TAEUBER, Karl E. and TAEUBER, Alma F. 'The Negro as an Immigrant Group: Recent Trends in Racial and Ethnic Segregation in Chicago', in *Racial and Ethnic Relations,* edited by Bernard E. Segal, Thomas Y. Crowell Company, New York, 1966.

VANN WOODWARD, C. *The Strange Career of Jim Crow.* Oxford University Press, London and New York, 1966.

WELDING, Pete. 'Homesick James Williamson', in *Blues Unlimited Collectors Classics 7* (May 1965).

Periodicals

Blues & Soul 90, 11-24 August 1972.
Blues Unlimited 76, October 1970.
   78, December 1970.
   84, September 1971.
Disc and Music Echo 15 January 1972.
Downbeat 7 August 1969.
Ebony August 1969.
Inbeat June 1967.
Look 14 July 1970.

Melody Maker 1 May 1971.
   2 October 1971.
   18 March 1972.
   6 May 1972.
   27 May, 1972.
   18 November 1972.
   16 December 1972.
   10 February 1973.
Newsweek 22 August 1966.
   24 July 1967
   7 August 1967.
   18 September 1967.
   26 May 1969.
   30 June 1969.
   29 July 1970.
R 'n' B World 17 October 1968.
Record World 10 August 1968.
   17 August 1968.
   24 August 1968.
Soul 3 June 1968.
   17 March 1969.
   22 September 1969.
Soul Sounds 31 October 1968.
Time 6 April 1970.
   9 August 1971.
   11 October 1971.

Television Programmes

BBC-TV 2, 'Sounds for Saturday', 22 July 1972.
Independent Television Network, 'Black Mayor', 6 July 1971.

Discography

Records referred to in the text which are listed in the two standard discographies—Godrich and Dixon: 1969 and Leadbitter and Slaven: 1968—are not included in this discography. Only single releases are included unless long playing records are specifically mentioned in the text. Data are confined to American releases.

James Barnes And The Agents	*Free At Last (Great Day A-Comin')*	Golden Hit Productions 101
Len Barry	*1–2–3*	Decca 31827
William Bell	*You Don't Miss Your Water*	Stax 116
Big Maybelle	*Keep That Man*	Rojac 116
Bobby Bland	*I'll Take Care of You*	Duke 314
	Lead Me On	Duke 318
	St. James' Infirmary	Duke 340
	Turn On Your Lovelight	Duke 344
	Yield Not to Temptation	Duke 352
	Stormy Monday	Duke 355
	That's the Way Love Is	Duke 360
	Call On Me	Duke 360
	The Feeling Is Gone	Duke 370
	That Did It	Duke 421
	Driftin' Blues	Duke 432
	Save Your Love For Me	Duke 435
Charles Brown	*I'm Gonna Push On*	Galaxy 766
	Black Night	King 6192
James Brown	*Please, Please, Please*	Federal 12258
	Shout And Shimmy	King 5657
	Papa's Got A Brand New Bag	King 5999
	I Feel Good	King 6015
	Don't Be A Dropout	King 6056
	I Got The Feeling	King 6155
	Say It Loud—I'm Black And I'm Proud	King 6187
	I Don't Want Nobody To Give Me Nothing	King 6224
	Get Up, Get Into It, Get Involved	King 6347
	King Heroin	Polydor 14116
	Public Enemy No. 1	Polydor 14153
Roy Brown	*Hard Luck Blues*	DeLuxe 3304
Mojo Buford	*It Was Early One Morning*	Adell 102
Solomon Burke	*Everybody Needs Somebody To Love*	Atlantic 2241
	Take Me Just As I Am	Atlantic 2416
Bobby Byrd	*If You Don't Work You Can't Eat*	King 6342
James Carr	*Freedom Train*	Goldwax 338
Clarence Carter	*Slip Away*	Atlantic 2508
Ray Charles	*I Got A Woman*	Atlantic 1050
	This Little Girl of Mine	Atlantic 1063
	Tell All The World About You	Atlantic 2010
	What'd I Say	Atlantic 2031
	Eleanor Rigby	ABC 11090
Sonny Charles	*Black Pearl*	A & M 1053
Chi—Lites	*Let Me Be The Man My Daddy Was*	Brunswick 755414
	Give More Power To The People	Brunswick 55450
Jimmy 'Soul' Clarke	*If Only I Knew Then*	Karen 1539
Tony Clarke	*Ghetto Man*	Chicory 409

Mitty Collier	Everybody Makes A	
	Mistake Sometime	Chess 2050
Arthur Connelly	People Sure Act Funny	Atco 6588
Sam Cooke	Let The Good Times Roll	RCA 8368
	A Change Is Gonna Come	RCA 8486
King Curtis	Soul Serenade	Atco 6511
	Memphis Soul Stew	Atco 6511
Dells	Freedom Means	Cadet 5683
Detroit Emeralds	(I'm An Ordinary Man) Take	
	Me The Way I Am	Ric Tic 141
Dramatics	The Devil Is Dope	Volt 4090
Dyke And The Blazers	We Got More Soul	Original Sound 86
Falcons	I Found A Love	Lupine 1003
Flamingoes	You Me And The Sea	End 1068
Eddie Floyd	Knock On Wood	Stax 194
	I've Never Found A Girl	Stax 0002
Aretha Franklin	Respect	Atlantic 2403
	Chain Of Fools	Atlantic 2464
	Since You've Been Gone	Atlantic 2486
	Think	Atlantic 2518
	You Send Me	Atlantic 2518
Getto Kitty	Hope For The Future	Stroud 55-05
Roscoe Gordon	Just A Little Bit	Vee Jay 332
Eddie Harris	Listen Here	Atlantic 2487
Dale Hawkins	Susie Q	Checker 863
Isaac Hayes	Theme From Shaft	Enterprise 9038
Willie Hightower	It's A Miracle	Capitol 2226
	Time Has Brought About	
	A Change	Fame 1474
Howling Wolf	Pop It To Me	Chess 2009
Impressions	It's Alright	ABC 10487
	Keep On Pushing	ABC 10544
	People Get Ready	ABC 10622
	We're A Winner	ABC 11022
	We're Rolling On	ABC 11071
Luther Ingram	You Can Depend On Me	Koko 2101
	To The Other Man	Koko 2106
Jesse James	Believe In Me Baby,	Twentieth
	Parts 1 and 2	Century Fox 6684
Syl Johnson	Come On, Sock It To Me	Twilight 100
	Different Strokes	Twilight 103
	Dresses Too Short	Twinight 110
	I Take Care Of Homework	Twinight 116
	Don't Give It Away	Twinight 118
	Is It Because I'm Black	Twinight 125
	We Do It Together	Twinight 144
	We Did It	Hi 2229
Albert King	Born Under A Bad Sign	Stax 217
B.B. King	Paying The Cost To Be The	
	Boss	Bluesway 61015
	I'm Gonna Do What They Do	
	To Me	Bluesway 61018
Frederick Knight	Lean On Me	Stax 0117
Little Milton	Blind Man	Checker 1096
	We're Gonna Make It	Checker 1105
	Dark End Of The Street	Checker 1203
	Grits Ain't Groceries	Checker 1212
	If That Ain't A Reason	Stax 0100
	Little Milton Sings Big Blues	
	(LP)	Checker 3002
Barbara Lynn	(Until Then) I'll Suffer	Atlantic 2812
Derek Martin	Soul Power	Volt 160
Amos Milburn	House Party	Aladdin 3306
Shan Miles	Soul People	Shout 222
Cliff Nobles	The Horse	Phil L.A. of Soul 313
Pace Setters	Push On Jesse Jackson	Kent 4565
Bobby Parker	Watch Your Step	V-Tone 223
Junior Parker	Five Long Years	Duke 306
	Driving Wheel	Duke 336
	Your Love's All Over Me	Mercury 72793

Junior Parker	*You Don't Have To Be Black*	
	To Love The Blues (LP)	Groove Merchant 502
Wilson Pickett	*In The Midnight Hour*	Atlantic 2289
Otis Redding	*Respect*	Volt 128
	The Happy Song (Dum Dum)	Volt 163
Otis Rush	*Gambler's Blues*	Cotillion 44032
Sam and Dave	*Soul Man*	Stax 231
	I Thank You	Stax 242
Moody Scott	*(We Gotta) Bust Out Of The*	
	Ghetto, Part 1	Sound Stage 7 2260
Marvin L. Simms	*Talkin' 'Bout Soul*	Revue 11024
Nina Simone	*Young, Gifted And Black*	RCA 0269
Staple Singers	*Respect Yourself*	Stax 0104
Candi Staton	*Stand By Your Man*	Fame 1472
Johnnie Taylor	*Next Time*	Stax 247
	Who's Makin' Love	Stax 0009
	Mr. Nobody Is Somebody	Stax 0055
	I Am Somebody, Parts 1	
	and 2	Stax 0078
Little Johnny Taylor	*Part Time Love*	Galaxy 722
	Everybody Knows About My	
	Good Thing, Part 1	Ronn 55
Temptations	*Ain't Too Proud To Beg*	Gordy 7054
	Please Return Your Love	
	To Me	Gordy 7074
Joe Tex	*A Woman's Hands*	Dial 4061
	Keep The One You've Got	Dial 4083
T.V. Slim	*Don't Knock The Blues*	Pzazz 005
Vontastics	*Day Tripper*	St. Lawrence 1014
Johnny Watson	*Soul Food*	Okeh 7290
Junior Wells	*Up In Heah*	Bright Star 149
	You're Tuff Enough	Blue Rock 4052
Larry Williams	*Short Fat Fanny*	Specialty 608
	Hootchy Koo	Specialty 634
	Bad Boy	Specialty 658
	She Said Yeah	Specialty 658
	Get Ready	Chess 1745
Jackie Wilson	*I Get The Sweetest Feeling*	Brunswick 55381
Winstons	*Color Him Father*	Metromedia 117
Stevie Wonder	*Where I'm Coming From*	
	(LP)	Tamla 308
	Music Of My Mind (LP)	Tamla 314
	Talking Book (LP)	Tamla 322
Young Rascals	*Groovin'*	Atlantic 2401

Song Credits

Every effort has been made to locate the copyright owners of the songs from which extracts are quoted in the text. Any omissions brought to our attention will be credited in subsequent printings. Grateful acknowledgement is made to the music publishers named for permission to quote from the songs listed below.

Back Door Friend by Lewis and Hopkins © 1968 Su-Ma Publishing Company, Inc. Used by permission.

Believe In Me Baby—Part 1 by James, Anderson, DeMell and DeSanto, published by Je-Ma Music Inc. and Shada Music Inc., recorded by Jesse James on 20th Century-Fox Records, recording produced by Jesse Mason Productions.

Believe In Me Baby—Part 2 by James, Thrower, Nelso, Crawford, Durio, published by Je-Ma Music Inc. and Shada Music Inc., recorded by Jesse James on 20th Century-Fox Records, recording produced by Jesse Mason Productions.

Blues Pain by Lowell Fulsom, published by Modern Music Publishing Co. Inc.

Born Under A Bad Sign © 1967 by East/Memphis Music Corp.

Bottle It Up And Go by Tommy McClennan, published by Wabash Music Company.

Don't Be A Dropout published by Intersong Music Ltd. (UK), Chappell & Co. Inc. (USA).

Down Don't Bother Me © 1966 by East Memphis Music Corp.

Feeling Awful Blues © Excellorec Music.

Five Long Years by Eddie Boyd © 1952 Frederick Music Company. Used by permission.

Ghetto Man by Tony Clarke and Roger Spotts © Copyright 1969 by Chicory Music Inc., Hollywood, California.

Freedom Train by Rogers, Wells and Bogart. With permission by Island Music Ltd. for UK, Eire, Australia and New Zealand. Published by Lyn-Lou Music Inc. (USA).

Hard Luck Blues published by Carlin Music Corporation.

I Don't Want Nobody To Give Me Nothing published by Intersong Music Ltd. (UK), Chappell & Co. Inc. (USA).

I Feel So Good published by USA Records Inc.

If I Only Knew Then (What I Know Now) by Richard Wylie and Anthony Hester. Copyright © 1968 by McLaughlin Pub. Co. and Ala King Music, 527 Madison Avenue, New York NY 10022.

If That Ain't A Reason (For Your Woman To Leave) © 1971 East/Memphis Music Corp. & Groovesville Music.

I'm Gonna Push On. Reproduced by kind permission of Burlington Music Co. Ltd., London, England.

It's Alright published by Curtom Publishing Co. Ltd.

Is It Because I'm Black published by Twinight Records Inc., and Hightone Publishers.

I Thank You © 1968 by Birdees Music Corp. and Walden Music.

I've Made Nights By Myself published by Carlin Music Corporation.

Keep On Pushing published by Curtom Publishing Co. Inc.

Mojo Hand by Lightnin' Hopkins. Copyright 1966, Irving Music Inc. (BMI). All Rights Reserved. Used by permission.

Next Time © 1968 by East/Memphis Music Corp.

Say It Loud, I'm Black And I'm Proud published by Intersong Music Ltd. (UK), Chappell & Co., Inc. (USA).

Slip Away published by Fame Publishing Co. Inc.

Soul Food published by April Music Ltd.

Soul Man © 1967 by Birdees Music Corp. and Walden Music.

The Happy Song (Dum Dum) © 1968 by East/Memphis Music and Time Music (USA), Carlin Music Corporation (UK).

Talkin' 'Bout Soul published by Anthor Music/Silver Fox Productions.

The Woman I Love by B.B. King and Joe Josea, published by Modern Music Publishing Co. Inc. and Sounds of Lucille Inc.

We Did It published by Jec Publishing Company.
(We Gotta) Bust Out Of The Ghetto published by Cape Ann Music Inc.
We're A Winner published by Curtom Publishing Co. Inc.
We're Gonna Make It published by Shada Music Inc.
We're Rolling On published by Curtom Publishing Co. Inc.
Who's Making Love © 1968 by East/Memphis Music Corp.
Why Do Everything Happen To Me by Roy Hawkins and Jules Taub, published by Modern Music Publishing Co. Inc.
Worry Worry by Plummer Davis and Jules Taub, published by Modern Music Publishing Co. Inc.
You Can Depend On Me by Luther Ingram. Copyright © 1968 by Klondike Enterprises Ltd, 527 Madison Avenue, New York NY 10022.

Picture Credits

Grateful acknowledgement is made to the photographers, copyright holders and owners listed below for permission to reproduce the photographs used in this book.

ABC/DUNHILL RECORDS   34, 160 (courtesy Sidney A. Seidenberg, Inc.), 170.
BOB ABRAMS AND ASSOCIATES   103
DICK ALAN MANAGEMENT, INC.   126 (courtesy Roy Simonds).
ASSOCIATED PRESS   139, 144.
ATLANTIC RECORDS   102, 155.
BUDDAH RECORDS   118, 134 (courtesy Roy Simonds), 172, 173.
CHESS RECORDS   75.
COLUMBIA PICTURES INDUSTRIES INC.   147 L, 147 R (courtesy Clive Richardson).
DUKE RECORDS   58, 73 L (courtesy Dan Kochakian).
BILL GREENSMITH   18, 19, 55, 84, 87.
GROOVE MERCHANT INTERNATIONAL INC.   73 R.
MICHAEL HARALAMBOS   12, 13, 14, 15, 52, 97, 98, 105, 109.
WILLIE HIGHTOWER   136.
IMPERIAL GROUP LTD.   47
PAUL OLIVER   132, 162.
ORIGINAL SOUND RECORDS   130.
POLYDOR RECORDS   Cover, 107, 122.
ANDRE SOUFFRONT   133 (courtesy 'Living Blues').
STAX RECORDS   22, 92, 114 L (courtesy Roy Simonds), 114 R (courtesy Paragon Agency), 140, 147 T (courtesy Roy Simonds), 171 L, 171 R, 171 B (Courtesy Chris Savory).
JEFF TITON   31 T, 63, 66, 88.
TVA   28 (courtesy Paul Oliver).
U.S. DEPARTMENT OF AGRICULTURE   31 B, 43, 44, 45 T, 45 C, 45 B, 46, 48, 49
WPA   36 (courtesy Paul Oliver).
WVON RADIO   85 L, 85 R.

Index

Haralambos, Michael
    Right on : from blues to soul in black
America / Michael Haralambos. - London :
Eddison Press, [1974]
    187 p. : ill.   592

    1. Negro music - History and criticism.
2. Blues (Songs,   etc.) - United States -
History and crit   icism. I.t.